PROFIT FIRST
FOR
REAL ESTATE AGENTS

PROFIT FIRST

FOR

REAL ESTATE AGENTS

DAMON YUDICHAK

Orange Star Press, LLC, Wake Forest, North Carolina

Published 2022
Printed in the United States of America

ISBN: 978-1-7378512-1-9 (trade paperback)
ISBN: 978-1-7378512-0-2 (eBook)

Page Design & Typesetting: Chinook Design, Inc. (chinooktype.com)
Cover design: Tehsin Gull

CONTENTS

To Nana, who lived the good life.
May your name be remembered for a blessing.

FOREWORD BY MIKE MICHALOWICZ

A s the event host approached us, Damon Yudichak said, "Leuk je te ontmoeten."

Don't worry, I don't know what that means either. In case you are not fluent in Dutch, it translates to "It is nice to meet you."

I had just delivered my Profit First keynote at ProfitCON Europe, an annual event held in the Amsterdam area of the Netherlands. Damon had flown in from the US for the event. He knew the system inside and out but wanted to experience its subtleties by observing different businesses in different countries that use Profit First.

We had just gone to break when Femke Hogema, the event host, came over to greet us. Femke smiled when she heard Damon's greeting, and they briefly chatted in Dutch punctuated with laughter.

"I didn't know you were fluent in Dutch," I said to Damon.

"Yeah. I lived here for a few years and studied the language. I love to immerse myself in different environments and learn everything." He chuckled and continued, "And the more I learn, the more I can serve."

Damon discovered Profit First when I first released the book. He immediately immersed himself in the system. He used it to turn his own struggling business into a success. And he did it in classic Yudichak style: complete immersion. He learned all the components of the system, enhanced elements to better serve himself, and became Profit First Mastery-certified. In other words, Damon mastered the "language" of Profit First.

Books can be spawned at the most unexpected times. Great ideas spring up in the shower. And, apparently, amazing real estate books spring up at conferences in the Netherlands. It was at this event that it struck him: With the proper "translation," Profit First could serve real estate agents.

Damon is in his second decade of serving real estate agents through his practice. He has guided more than eight hundred agents to stronger, healthier, and permanently profitable businesses. From brand-new agents selling their first homes to agents moving hundreds of properties a year—and everyone in between—Damon has served them all. And now he will serve you.

After Femke moved on to greet the hundreds of other guests at the event, Damon and I continued to talk. And that is when he told me about his idea.

"Real estate agents need a version of *Profit First* specifically written for them. And I am the guy to write it," Damon said.

At that moment, this book was born. Damon and I had the agreement in place by the weekend, and for the next two years, he painstakingly enhanced the Profit First system for real estate agents. For you. You hold the results in your hands right now. This book, *Profit First for Real Estate Agents*, is a masterful translation and enhancement of the Profit First system specifically for you and your agency.

Money is one of the least understood and most confusing subjects for real estate agents. It is bewildering to be responsible for the transfer of so much money—with allocations to so many different entities—and yet, at the end of the day, it seems there is little (or none) left for you. Why is that?

In *Profit First for Real Estate Agents*, you will master the simple Profit First money management system. It will transform your business into one that is permanently profitable. And it will do that is because it works with your behaviors. You won't need to change; the system around you will change to match your needs.

Profitability is closer and easier than you imagine—you just need the right system. Damon will walk you through it, hand in hand. He will show you how to navigate the spikes and sags of a commission-earned income so you don't experience the feast-or-famine cycle that's all too common for real estate agents. He will show you why selling more homes may actually worsen your financials, and what to do to instantly remedy that. And he will show you how to both make more and take more, permanently.

The opportunity to have a successful, profitable real estate business is more accessible than ever before. But the journey is also more perilous. Technology is causing a massive shift in the industry. Agents who have the money to leverage it will be more successful. The ones who don't will, sadly, be swept away.

This is a moment of choice for you. Let the advancing industry have its way with you—or master money and grow. Since you are reading this book, it is clear which path you have chosen: the latter. You are ready to master money. And I can tell you from my own experience that when you have consistent profits, the stress goes away. You can plan and strategize better. You can move faster. You can lead an industry. And you can define the lifestyle you want.

You are moments away from a life-transforming experience. So let's not dillydally. Let's read!

Mike Michalowicz
Boonton, New Jersey

CHAPTER 1:

IT'S ALL ABOUT THE MONEY

Sally waited tables before she started her career in real estate. She didn't finish college. Maybe real estate was a way to get ahead. She was pregnant, just weeks away from single motherhood, but after hours of serving hangry guests, she gave her swollen feet a rest at real estate school. She sat at a desk designed for people without pregnant bellies. She passed her real estate license exam and got a job as an agent for a local builder. The job gave her the stability she needed, but she only sold houses when people came to the specific neighborhood where the builder worked, and where Sally and her daughter lived. Soon, Sally become frustrated and quit the real estate game because she didn't see enough opportunity for her precious daughter in the area.

George left a safe government job where he served his community for twenty years. With his high energy, hard work, and tenacity, he then built a successful real estate team. He is now in his second decade as an agent. He averages $300 million in annual sales, but things are different now: The marketing he did five years ago with his team of ten agents doesn't work the way it used to, and it is much more expensive to find qualified buyers and sellers. In the last six months, George lost half of his team of agents. He fired some of them because they didn't have the discipline to lead-generate each day. Those bottom-feeders relied on George to give them all their leads. The other agents left George for another team that boasted of its "greener pastures."

Scott is overwhelmed. He works more than he desires to. Each night after dinner with his family, he rushes to show another house. He feels as if he is on a hamster wheel. He is torn between the work he loves and guilt about how little time he spends with his wife and their children. He sold eighty houses last year, yet he worries and wonders why he struggles to make his car payment.

Bruce and Steve have been together for more than twenty-five years. Bruce is a full-time real estate agent, while Steve, a full-time corporate accountant, supports Bruce with administrative tasks on the weekends. They both make good money but are so involved in their work lives, they don't take much time off for themselves. Bruce gives until he's so depleted that he desperately needs time away. Every year, the couple goes on a seven-day destination vacation to recharge and get some relief from their busy lives. Each time, Steve tolerates the phone calls and emails Bruce answers as he tries to save yet another home sale at risk of not closing. Bruce questions why there are more emergencies now than when he first started.

Shameka wishes things could be simpler. Why does life have to be so hectic? She juggles too many things. There is never enough time. She often feels trapped and doesn't think there is a way out. *My finances are a huge mess. I don't know where to start.* She hired Bob, an accountant, but every time he talks, her eyes gloss over. *Whoosh* is the sound she hears as all those words from Bob fly over her head. *I'll never understand this money thing.* She goes back to her default solution: *I just need to sell one more house. That will solve all my problems.*

Each of these successful real estate agents is haunted by something off-kilter in their business. Something isn't quite right. They lead-generate and hit their transaction goals, and yet a gnawing unease wakes them in the middle of the night. Maybe at two a.m., like me. Maybe three. Maybe they're up all night. Their minds jump like gazelles chased by lions. Overthinking ensues. Then overwhelm. They've hired coaches who helped them break through limiting beliefs and self-doubt. They seek guidance from their mentors. But no matter how much good advice they get, their restlessness continues to swirl beneath the surface.

Maybe you feel a similar anxiety and frustration. Does your business make a lot of money, yet you question where it all goes? Are you shocked when you receive your 1099 in January and see your total income for the year? You look at your bank account, bewildered by how little money remains; you exceeded your transaction goals but seem to have nothing to show for it. What about taxes? Why can't your accountant keep you from those dreaded tax surprises each year? Now you have to scramble to sell a few more houses so you can pay Uncle Sam or, worse yet, you have to go on a payment plan. You may worry that you'll rot in tax jail.

If you are like some of the real estate agents I've come to know over my thirteen-plus years in business, you love what you do. You help people find their dream homes. The real estate industry enables you to build something for yourself, to take advantage of opportunities you would never have had as an employee.

And yet here you are…

Successful at selling, yet money-challenged.

What if I told you that money is a game with simple rules? If you're not having fun with your money, it may be that the game is playing you rather than you playing it.

THE DEVIOUS DUO

In this game, you'll embark on a heroic journey fraught with villains and obstacles along the way—but also promising a pot of gold. You are the hero who will build something from nothing.

Before you start the journey, I'll need to introduce you to The Devious Duo. If you have ever struggled with money, you may be confused by where it goes. These two are responsible for most of your money woes. Their mission is to separate you from your gold.

Bonnie is a cute red squirrel. Her code name is The Distractor. She'll do whatever she can to misdirect you from what is important. At first glance, she appears to be innocent. She'll bat her eyes at you. She'll sing out your name and shout, "Look over here!" She prances and dances around with glee; she lives in the world of fun, excitement, and flash. Don't be fooled. She is a master of distraction. Her primary job is to ensnare you in a diversion so her partner can slip his wily little hands into your pockets.

Clyde, her partner, is a raccoon with a fat bank account padded with wealth from those he has swindled. He wears the bandit's mask. No one is immune to him. His code name is The Human Problem. The only thing you'll hear him say is, "Spend everything you make!" Sometimes he'll sneak up behind you and whisper this in your ear. At others he'll shout it from the rooftops. The constant drumbeat of his mantra has trapped much of humanity in a cycle of living paycheck to paycheck.

Bonnie and Clyde prey on humans because they are the only ones who have money. The Devious Duo are master thieves and have spent thousands of years perfecting their craft. You must protect yourself from them, or they will get to you when you least expect it. When times are tough, they'll tempt you with get-rich-quick schemes. When you live high off the hog, they'll lull you into complacency and convince you that the good times will never end. You may buy into their lie, that the constant flow of gold will never cease. While they appear cuddly, don't let them get too close. They are tree rats who will poison you with poverty.

THE GAME YOU'VE BEEN PLAYING IS RIGGED AGAINST YOU

It's not your fault you aren't a millionaire yet. Bonnie and Clyde tricked you into playing the wrong game—one designed to make other people rich, not you; one focused primarily on sales as the key to a successful real estate business. Bonnie uses her web of lies to convince you it takes money to make money; meanwhile, Clyde urges you to spend, spend, and spend some more. While you run around in circles, as chasing your tail, Bonnie and Clyde laugh at you until you end up broke and alone.

It's time to leave their game behind and play one designed with your best interests in mind—one that is simple to understand and will provide you with predictable results while giving you the power to control your income and lifestyle.

If you want better results with your money, then this book is for you. We'll begin with the fundamentals so you have a solid foundation. Step by step, we'll build a money system that makes sense to you. If you want a permanent solution to your financial worries, then this is your guide to a better financial future.

When you read and apply the money principles in these pages, your life will change. You'll have the money to live your dreams, whatever they may be. Pay off the soul-sucking debt. Fund your children's education. Have a cash cushion so you can breathe easily when emergencies arise. You deserve to live your life to the fullest.

You are the best person to improve your finances. If you're looking for someone to save you without you putting in the effort, this book will not help you. Change is possible for you now. Be open. Trust the process and commit to improving your business and your life. You will get immediate results with your very next deposit.

You won't become rich overnight, but you can stop digging a financial hole to nowhere overnight. Next, you'll fill in the hole. Then you'll build your riches. It is a process. It will take time. When you take the right actions, you will get the right results. When you get the right results, you will get excited about your life and your future. Success breeds success and success becomes its own reward.

DON'T TREAT YOUR BUSINESS LIKE A LOTTERY TICKET

Did you know that every day, more than 125,000 people cross the Brooklyn Bridge? If you charged a toll of one dollar for every person who crossed the bridge, you would earn more than $44 million each year. That's a nice sum. Back in his day, George C. Parker claimed to have the rights to sell the Brooklyn Bridge. He approached new immigrants as they entered New York City and told them about a fantastic business opportunity. Some were defrauded by his shenanigans. Finally, the law caught up with him and he spent the last years of his life incarcerated at Sing Sing Correctional Facility.

Getting rich in America is the ultimate American dream. Nothing is so powerful in America as the desire to strike it rich. The Gold Rush of 1848 brought tens of thousands of prospectors to Northern California in search of untold fortune. The very founding of America was fueled by those who sought wealth.

If history is any indication of the future, most who start a real estate career will fail within five years of getting their license. I was headed down the path of failure when I started my accounting business more than thirteen years ago.

Where do people go wrong? They think that the next home sale will be the salvation of their business. It never is. As your business grows, it will become more expensive to run. With every new dollar you earn, less will belong to you. Then Clyde, The Human Problem, will sneak up behind you and rasp in your ear, "Spend everything you make."

We've been told over and over again that more sales will solve all our problems. This is one of the lies that Bonnie, The Distractor, spreads to divert us from the root causes of our money woes. More sales are only valuable if they are profitable sales, meaning you keep more money than you spend. I've known people who lose money when they make a sale. Think about this for a moment. You sell something and you lose money in the process. Do this too often and additional sales lead to getting further behind.

The most effective long-term strategy for building your real estate business is to grow and nurture a solid database of people. It takes time and effort to build relationships with the people in your database. You've got to keep in touch with them. Make phone calls, host events and show you care about them. The work you do now may take a couple months or years to pay off, but it will.

You know what doesn't take a lot of work? Spending a boatload of money on marketing. All these marketing companies tell tall tales about the exponential growth you'll see with their fancy-schmancy solutions. It's as if they want to sell you the Brooklyn Bridge. They tell you all you need to do is sell just one additional house and it will pay for itself. They whet your appetite with their bright, shiny silver bullet. Excitement boils up. Maybe all your woes will be gone forever. You throw caution to the wind and spend too much to market for new clients. Then you end up with a millstone around your neck, growing to feed the beast of marketing for growth's sake alone. This is growth without the fundamentals of profitability, good money piled on after bad. Many have mistakenly believed that if they just grew, the profits would suddenly appear. They never do. It's not how much you make that is important. What is important is how much money you keep.

Many people overestimate what they can accomplish in one year and underestimate what they can accomplish in five years. We live in an instant gratification bubble where we think we can plant a seed today and reap the crop tomorrow. This kind of thinking is disastrous for our long-term success. Recognize and accept that there is a growth season for everything. If we want true long-term success, we must do the hard work essential to achieving success and our objectives. Give your work a chance to sprout, grow, and bear fruit. If you constantly pluck it out of the ground to examine the roots, you will never taste that fruit.

THE TWO MISSING PUZZLE PIECES

In his transformative book *The Richest Man in Babylon*, George S. Clason wrote, "If you have not acquired more than a bare existence in the years since we were youths, it is because you either have failed to learn the laws that govern the building of wealth, or else you do not observe them."[1]

I rephrase Clason's words as follows: "If you haven't built wealth since you started your business, either you don't know the money laws or you fail to follow them."

Look at your bank account and answer this simple question: Are you happy with the balance? If the answer is yes, I congratulate you. If the answer is no, it's time to try a different approach. It's time to improve your knowledge and your actions.

Here's the good news: Unlike Bonnie and Clyde's complex and convoluted game, you'll play this one with easy-to-understand instructions built upon a few simple habits. You won't be bombarded by the confusing noise Bonnie shouts at you through her megaphone. Here are some common misconceptions she chimes at you:

- You can't be rich without debt.
- All you need to do to solve your problems is earn more money.
- You can buy your way to success.
- A large income will keep you out of debt.
- More money will give you happiness.
- Everything will work itself out.
- You don't need discipline to be rich.
- You just need one big payday and all your money woes will be solved.
- Just sell one more house.

---

[1] George S. Clason, *The Richest Man in Babylon* (New York, NY: Hawthorn, 1955).

How many of these lies have you been duped into believing? I've only listed nine. I could add at least a thousand more to the list.

To simplify money, we need to approach our finances as we would a messy room. If we try to clean the room in one fell swoop, we will wear ourselves out. What if we committed to five minutes of work per day on the room? Can you commit to five minutes? Sure you can. When you watch TV and a commercial comes on, stand up and clean the room. Day after day, you will remove the junk and clean the room. Small actions taken daily lead to big results.

While there are many principles of financial success, some are more important than others. In fact, if you can focus on only two, they will give you the biggest bang for your buck. Does that seem doable? How easy would your life be if you only had to focus on two things? These two golden keys are:

- **Pay yourself first.**
- **Spend less than you earn.**

When you use these two keys and commit to them for the rest of your life, your finances will improve dramatically. The nirvana you will achieve is a land where you no longer worry about money.

If you want more cash in your bank now, it's time to leave Bonnie and Clyde behind. They've given you nothing but trouble while you toiled away, grinding your fingers to the bone. They've kept you trapped in a fool's game. It doesn't matter if you did the best you could; their game will always be rigged, and it is next to impossible to succeed when the system is rigged against you. Now is the time to make a positive change in your life that will reward you and your loved ones for the remainder of your days.

In this book, I give you the same proven system I developed over many years to gain control of my money. When I first met with Crystal, she told me her money anxiety was sky-high. She worried constantly about how she was going to make ends meet. Four weeks later, after she had begun implementing the system, I asked what her money anxiety level was. She replied, "It's about a three now when it was an eight a few weeks ago. I have more clarity and am not nearly as worried about money as I was when we first met."

This system enables my real estate clients to get a handle on their business and personal expenses. They come to me in desperation and emerge knowing what it takes to successfully operate their real estate businesses. They cover all the bases and set aside money for their taxes.

The system works if you work it. It is built on a few steps. They will move you closer to financial abundance.

MONEY SUCCESS IS SIMPLER THAN MOST PEOPLE REALIZE

When it comes to your business money, the success formula is a cinch.

INCOME > SPENDING = SUCCESS

INCOME < SPENDING = FAILURE

Remember, the two golden keys of money are:

- **Pay yourself first.**
- **Spend less than you earn.**

If you always pay yourself first, you reward yourself for your hard work. Admit it: You work hard. You deserve to be paid fairly. Embrace everything you do for your business. Reward yourself for your commitment to excellence. You give everything to your life's work.

When you spend less than you earn, you will never run out of money. Because this concept is so important, I want you to read it again. When you spend less than you earn, you will never run out of money. Now close your eyes and repeat after me: When you spend less than you earn, you will never run out of money.

What are the two golden keys of money?

- **Pay yourself first.**
- **Spend less than you earn.**

I don't care how bad your finances are right now. Life gets in the way and we don't always make the best decisions. No matter where you are now, your financial and business future are a clean slate. You can use the power of your daily decisions and actions to chart a new path for yourself—a new path where money is no longer a source of stress, but a wellspring of hope and security.

YOUR BUSINESS IS YOUR BEST CHANCE TO WIN WITH MONEY

You owe it to yourself to become a master of your money. The only reason to be in business is to make the money to live your dream life. When you work for someone else, they will always have some control over your destiny.

Chances are, you will spend the next ten years of your life working. Think back to where you were ten years ago. Are you better off financially than you were then? What do you want your life to be ten years from now? Are you ready for a better life, filled with more abundance? If you can dream it, you can achieve it—but only if you use the right systems.

To achieve your dreams, you'll need three things:

- Knowledge about what the dream is
- Knowledge about what it takes to achieve the dream
- Some money

Let's start with something small. Answer the following question:

If you could improve one thing about your financial situation, what would it be?

Now it's time to do a little math. Yes, you will have to do a bit of math, but don't fret, I'll keep it simple. I want you to develop a target for what you can achieve when you apply this book's principles in your business.

Look at your 1099 from last year and you will see the total commissions you earned. Multiply your total gross commission income (GCI) by 10% (e.g., total GCI = $100,000 × 10% = $10,000).

What would you do if you had an extra $10,000 in your bank account right now?

For many people, $10,000 would make a big difference. If you apply the steps I share with you in this book, you will have more money in your bank account in twelve months than you do now.

Most real estate agents know how much income they make. Most people focus on more sales as the cure for their financial woes. The challenge with this approach is that, in most cases, every new sale leads to more work. That sounds great. We want more work. If you are good at what you do and promote yourself properly, you will attract new business. Eventually, you will run into a capacity issue. Then you will run out of time. When you run out of time, you have the following three options:

- Add more capacity by hiring employees, vendors, or independent contractors
- Keep capacity constant, which means placing a ceiling on earnings
- Reduce capacity, which means making less money

How would you feel if you were overworked and still didn't have enough to make ends meet? You'd be like a one-legged mule in a butt-kicking contest, working yourself to the bone and yet having nothing to show for it. This is the result many people experience when the only thing they focus on is growing sales.

If you can't make money to support yourself selling thirty homes per year, you will be unable to support yourself selling three hundred homes per year. The best way to be more profitable later is to be more profitable now. You must nail profitability down right now, at your current sales volume, because everything becomes more expensive as your business grows.

TAKE ACTION: SEND ME AN EMAIL

It's time to draw a line in the sand and have some accountability. Email me right now at Damon@idealmoneylife.com with the subject line "My $10,000" and tell me what you would do with an extra $10,000. If you are all in on this, I want to know it. Email me. Commit. Let's do this.

CHAPTER 2:

GET REAL ABOUT MONEY

When I was in middle school, I played basketball almost every day with my best friend Jeremy.

I recall a particular game of twenty-one and the feel of the bump-covered surface of the ball as I pushed it down with my right hand and how, just like a yo-yo, it returned to my palm moments later. I danced around Jeremy and grabbed the ball with both hands. I glanced at the orange rim. I was in the clear. Jump. Release. Swoosh. My arms went up in celebration. I had just scored three in a row. I was on a run. *Can I outwit and outmaneuver?*

Jeremy blocked my next shot. He scored twice. We were tied—do or die. *Will I get the bragging rights?*

Then Jeremy reached in, stole the ball, and took a jump shot. The ball crawled through the air as if in slow motion and bounced off the backboard. It swirled around the rim. *Dooooon't gooooooo innnnnnnn!*

But it did. I frowned. Jeremy had won. I gave him a high five. Time to head home for dinner.

"Tomorrow, I'll wear the crown!" I declared as I left.

"I'll believe it when I see it."

Try as I might, I never mastered the skyhook. I would never be Kareem Abdul-Jabbar, the Hall of Fame player, but

I had fun. I thought I was good enough for my high school team. However, after a week of tryouts, my basketball "career" was over. I didn't make the cut. My name wasn't on the list for the second round. If only I'd had Kareem's two extra vertical feet.

In his book *Coach Wooden and Me: Our 50-Year Friendship On and Off the Court*, Kareem Abdul-Jabbar shares the experience of his first day of practice at UCLA. Coach John Wooden had just won his second straight NCAA championship. A mix of veteran and new players circled around Coach. A new adventure. How would it begin?

Coach Wooden said, "Good afternoon, gentlemen. Today we are going to learn how to put on our sneakers and socks correctly."

Put on our shoes, you've got to be kidding me! thought Kareem.

This wasn't Kareem's first day at the rodeo. He was a dominant high school All-American. He knew a thing or two about how to throw an orange ball through a hoop. He had come to the City of Angels to learn at the great John Wooden's feet. He just didn't know that would be literal.

Coach Wooden continued his instructions. "If you do not pull your socks on tightly, you're likely to get wrinkles in them. Wrinkles cause blisters. Blisters force players to sit on the sidelines. And players sitting on the sidelines lose games. So we are not just going to tug. We are also going to make it snug."[2]

Every year, Coach Wooden started the first practice of the season with this same lesson. His methods speak for themselves. He won ten NCAA championships during his twelve-year tenure as UCLA's head coach. The team's roster was full of the

---

[2] Kareem Abdul-Jabbar, *Coach Wooden and Me: Our 50-year Friendship On and Off the Court* (New York, NY: Grand Central Publishing, 2017).

nation's best and brightest college players. It didn't matter to Wooden. They were on his court. He needed to reinforce the fundamentals. He knew he couldn't build a championship team without a solid foundation.

Many of the clients I work with are super successful. They inspire me. Yet they come to me because they are confused about their money. Money is one of the most complex, intimate topics people face. When someone talks to me about it, they share a deep part of their soul. It bothers me that people work so hard to achieve success and struggle with money. Why does it have to be so complicated? I used to think it wasn't rocket science. Maybe not for me; I spent a few decades working in finance. For most people, though, money *is* rocket science. If you are confused by money, you are not alone. Most are challenged by it because it's a complex, tangled, bewildering mess. It needs to be made simpler so people can understand it.

Let's follow Coach Wooden's example and build your championship business. Let's learn how to put on your business's socks so you aren't sidelined by those pesky wrinkles. You're in this game for the long haul. You don't have time to bother with those silly little blisters.

Take the advice of Gary Keller, coauthor of *The Millionaire Real Estate Agent*, and focus on one thing.[3] Sure, you help people find their dream homes. You build a team. You solve problems. You can list plenty of reasons why you love your profession. While those are nice, you must never forget the primary reason you own a business.

You are in business to make money.

---

[3] Gary Keller, Dave Jenks, Jay Papasan, and Kyle Hebert, *The Millionaire Real Estate Agent* (Austin, TX: Millionaire Systems, 2006).

You've made tremendous investments of time, energy, resources, and money. What a waste it would be if you didn't earn a fabulous return on your investment. You deserve to be paid lots of money for your investments.

Money is at the core of everything you do, from the moment you pick up your phone to lead-generate to the moment you smile proudly as your client signs the closing documents for the home they've carefully saved up for. If money isn't important to you, then it might be time to choose a different profession. The demands of business are too great for someone who isn't in this for the greenbacks. If you don't focus on making money, you're better off with a job that just pays your bills. Become a master of money if you want to be successful with it. Otherwise, you'll suffer needlessly.

Pause for a moment. Breathe in once. Breathe out once. Breathe in again. Breathe out again. Now say these words aloud with as much conviction as you can muster:

I am in business to make money.

Remember how Coach Wooden started the first practice of the season with a lesson for his players to put on their shoes and socks? These were the best and brightest players in the country. Yet he took valuable time to start where the rubber of their soles met the court's wooden floor. Mastering the fundamentals was of utmost importance to him.

We will take the same approach with your business. You're already successful at selling. Yet if you struggle with money, chances are you need to get back to the basics of money. I'll guide you toward mastering it, and we will start with the fundamentals. The path to mastery follows a natural progression. You must develop disciplines, learn skills, try something new, and fail a few times. You'll be horrible at first. Then you'll be bad. Next, you'll be adequate—until you progress to good, great, and then excellent. There is no shortcut to mastery. You can't start off bad and become great overnight. It will take some effort and time.

BUSINESS SUCCESS EQUALS PROFIT

While the 2019-2020 official rulebook of the National Basketball Association is more than ninety pages long, you don't need to read the book to determine who is winning. The team with the most points is in the lead. How do you get more points? Throw an orange ball through the hoop. Do this more than your opponent and you will win the game. Part of the reason why people enjoy basketball is because it's easy to know how to win. You will bring the same simplicity to your real estate business when you focus on how to win.

Each morning, I go for a walk. Some days I see a copper coin on the ground with Abraham Lincoln's head emblazoned on it. I bend over and claim ownership of my newfound wealth. When I get home, I place it in an old glass Mt. Olive pickle jar. The green screw-on top has a slit in it. Clink. My heart jumps a bit every time I hear that music.

I respect money and have a special place for all my precious coins. Some people have so little awareness about their money, they let it slip through their hands and drive over it with their cars. You might think, *It's only a penny, Damon.* No, you're wrong: it's a principle. Small, wasteful indiscretions are indicative of larger waste.

One morning, I found five pennies.

"Jackpot!" I proclaimed.

Five pennies on my walk. I made a profit. Profit is so simple. More money at the end than at the beginning.

Without profit, you do not have a business. You have an expensive hobby.

Imagine you're in your car. Trees line the sidewalk. You see a young girl at the side of the road with a lemonade stand and realize your mouth is dry. You look at the car's dashboard. Ninety-two degrees. You park your car and walk over to quench your thirst. It's been a mere thirty seconds, yet a bead of sweat dribbles down your forehead and into your right eye.

"Hello, my name is Norah! Do you want a cup of lemonade? It's just fifty cents!"

"I want two cups." You smile, reach into your pocket and hand over a crisp one-dollar bill. Norah has blue eyes and bobbed brown hair that falls to her jawline.

At the top of the stand is a handwritten sign: "Lemonade 50¢ a cup." The magic elixir is a concoction of lemon juice, water, and sugar. Each cup has a price of just two quarters; a fair exchange of money for a product. Norah spent less than five cents on the ingredients. Fifty cents income minus five cents cost equals forty-five cents profit. Presto. Earnings less expenses equal profit. It's hard to mess up business when you simplify it to its core.

Norah captured the simplicity of business that we, as adults, overcomplicate. We tangle it up in such a mess that we don't know if we have a cat or a ball of yarn.

Think about the simplicity of your own business. When you sell a home, you get paid a percentage commission of the sale. What a simple way to price your services. You don't have to worry about billable hours. When your client signs a listing contract, they know exactly what they pay you when the house sells. You know how much you will make. Everything is clear.

Profit is the primary goal of business. Don't lose sight of that. Otherwise, you'll veer off the path and head into the woods of confusion, where you'll trip over roots. You face enough challenges. You don't need money to be difficult. You need it to be simple. What if you had an easy button for your money? Your number one goal is cash. Period.

Profit is also known as cash in the bank. If you don't have cash in the bank, your business is not profitable. Cash in the bank is the only indicator of profit that matters. Your goal should be to have more money in the bank at the end of each month than you had at the beginning of each month. Is your bank account anemic? Focus on more profits.

The rest of this book gives you my proven profit system for your real estate business. You'll gain new insights into how money works. I'll translate all the fancy-schmancy business mumbo jumbo into plain English so you can explain it to a second grader. If a little girl like Norah knows how money works, just think how much better you can do with yours. I'll give you simple actions you can take today to grow cash in your bank accounts. Follow the system and you will get better with money.

WHY DO WE STRUGGLE WITH MONEY?

Every geographic area is prone to natural disasters. California has its earthquakes. Florida has hurricanes. Dorothy from *The Wizard of Oz* lived in Kansas, where her house was sucked up by a tornado. No matter where you live, there is the risk that nature will bring havoc into your life.

When it comes to money, everyone has challenges. People who don't have enough struggle to make ends meet. People who make a lot are bewildered by where all the money went. Many real estate agents worry about where their next commission check will come from.

One of my long-time clients referred Jasmine to me. Jasmine finished her second year in real estate having sold forty-three houses. When she came into my office, her face was flushed.

Her hands were restless. She blurted out, "Just when I thought I was getting ahead, my old accountant finished my tax returns and now I owe a bunch of money. It will empty out my bank account. What am I supposed to do? I heard there are all these write-offs for real estate agents, but my accountant didn't help me lower my tax bill. I asked him what I could do to lower it, and he spouted all this jargon. I could hear my brain cells scream as they drowned in a flood of details. Why does it have to be so complicated?"

I responded, "What confuses you?"

"No matter how much I make, there never seems to be enough."

"I hear that all the time. Everyone fights with what I call 'the human problem.' We spend as much as we make. I see it in everyone I work with. I battle with it. We spend everything we make. Unless we have a simple system to protect us from the human problem, we fall victim to it. None of us are robots. If we were robots, we would be immune to it. Unless you want the Wicked Witch of the West to turn you into the Tin Man and live without a heart, you will need to learn how to deal with the human problem."

Think about a house you currently have under contract. Lightning could strike the roof and set it on fire. To protect themselves from that risk, people buy insurance and pay taxes to fund fire departments. Over hundreds of years, municipalities enacted building codes for safety and to minimize damage from faulty wiring, lead-based paint, and water damage. We learn from disasters and—if we are wise—figure out ways to prevent them in the future.

In Chapter 1, I introduced you to The Devious Duo—Bonnie and Clyde. Bonnie will do everything she can to distract you. She knows that if she can, you will forget that profitability is the key to business success. Her partner, Clyde, will continually tell you to spend everything you make. If you struggle with money, you may not have a working system to combat and keep you safe from The Devious Duo.

MONEY IS THE MOST EMOTIONALLY CHARGED SUBJECT FOR US MORTALS

When our white Chevy Astro van pulled up to the church, I didn't want to get out. But it wasn't an option. My single mother, who raised me and my three siblings alone, told us, "We have to earn our keep."

Our job that day was to weed the flower beds around our church in exchange for the milk, canned goods, and other welfare food we received. The food was a godsend, but a part of me hated it. I wanted to be normal. I didn't want to be the kid on welfare. And I didn't want to miss out on playing basketball with my friends.

In the hot summer sun, I weeded and trimmed hedges. Bullets of sweat poured down my forehead and my T-shirt was drenched. Every thirty minutes or so, I went inside the church to get some cold water from the drinking fountain. As soon as I opened the door, a refreshing blast of cold enveloped me.

An hour or so into my work, Mr. Jones approached me. He was a tall, dapper man who showed up twenty-five minutes early to church every Sunday.

"Damon," he said, "thank you for all you're doing to make our church look beautiful. I'm impressed by your service!"

I smiled and nodded, but inside I was mortified. *Does he know we're on welfare?* My eyes darted around the church grounds. *Does everyone know?*

You may not want anyone else to know your financial realities, either—even the people you love or the people who depend on you.

Maybe your parents taught you more about money than mine did. The best thing I learned about it from them was that I didn't want my parents' lives. I didn't want to live in a world of need and deprivation. I wanted more. I instinctively knew that life was abundant. And I knew that if I could just learn how money worked, I would be successful with it.

When some people look at their bank accounts, it can be easy for them to see all their failures, excuses, should-haves, could-haves, and would-haves. We look into a mirror and straight at all our warts, skin tags, wrinkles, and flab. We judge ourselves and don't give ourselves enough grace. It's okay. The past is the past. You can't do anything about it now. No matter where you are now or where you've been, you did the best you could do with what you had and with what you knew. Own that now. You did your best. It's time to move on and create a better future. What is more important now is what you will choose to do today.

THE TWO REASONS WE FAIL WITH MONEY

My single mother toiled away at two jobs to make ends meet. She attended night school to get her teaching certification in the hopes of earning enough money that we wouldn't have to be on welfare anymore. It bothered me to see her struggle with money. As a teenager, I vowed that I would be the one to break the poverty cycle. I wouldn't allow the lack of money to limit me.

To help her make ends meet, my sister and I woke around two o'clock each morning to deliver *The Fayetteville Observer*. As soon as we finished the newspaper route, we showered and scurried off to school. Several times a week while at school, my head smacked against the table portion of my school desk. Those early mornings stretched me thin. I didn't let it faze me. I needed to study hard so I could earn a college scholarship. It was my best option to ensure that my future would change for the better.

My mother did the best she could, but the only thing my siblings and I knew about money was that there was never enough. She couldn't teach us how to be good with it. If she knew more about money, we would have had better lives than we did. I needed to figure it out on my own.

With every newspaper I threw, I built a bonfire deep within. I fed the fire with logs of discontent, shame, and deprivation. *Other people are rich—why can't I be?* I knew that money was the problem. We didn't have to be poor. I knew people who were well off and some who were rich. Their lives appeared to be better. They didn't have to struggle with a lack of money. If other people could have enough, then I was certain I could have enough as well.

I'd endured poverty for too long to allow myself to repeat those lean years as an adult. I knew I could choose a different path. The problem I had back then was, I didn't know what the path to prosperity looked like. However, I knew that somewhere, somehow, I would find the path if I kept at it. I was a student of money, and I needed a teacher.

Little did I know the teacher would be a man who had died about forty years earlier. He was a former mapmaker who began publishing financial advice pamphlets. In 1926, George S. Clason compiled those pamphlets into one of the best books on money ever written, *The Richest Man in Babylon*. The following words changed my life.

"If you have not acquired more than a bare existence in the years since we were youths, it is because you either have failed to learn the laws that govern the building of wealth, or else you do not observe them."[4]

This is the simplest explanation for a lack of money. There are two causes: Either one does not understand the laws of money, or one does not obey the laws of money.

When I read Clason's words, I knew I'd found the answers I'd been searching for. I decided I would not be a fool who spent his life confined to a bare existence. I would do everything I could to apply Clason's timeless wisdom to my life and no longer wander around in a financial wasteland.

MONEY IS MORE ABOUT BEHAVIOR THAN NUMBERS

Kareem Abdul-Jabbar holds the record for the most career points scored at 38,307. During his twenty-year professional career, he played 1,560 games. The key to so many points was the fact he played so many games. It's hard to score points when one isn't on the court.

Your long-term profit depends on your habits. My favorite quote about money comes from Benjamin Franklin. He said, "Your net worth to the world is usually determined by what remains after your bad habits are subtracted from your good ones."[5]

The most powerful action mechanism known to humanity is the humble habit. Imagine yourself in a chair outside. You feel the warmth from the sun as it caresses your face. Stand and look up at the sky. The vast blue is dotted with white puffy clouds.

Now look down. In front of you is the Grand Canyon, with its layered bands of red rock. Your breath catches as you take

---

[4] Clason, *Richest Man in Babylon*.

[5] Benjamin Franklin Quotes," BrainyQuote.com, accessed October 16, 2021, https://www.brainyquote.com/quotes/benjamin_franklin_151624.

in the majestic canyon. At its bottom, you see the blue water of the Colorado River. It has traveled along its path and carved the earth over millions of years. Consistently, day after day, water has moved along the riverbed to create a natural wonder.

When we harness the power of habits in our lives and to achieve our goals, we have the same power as the Colorado River, slowly carving its way through what is now the southwestern United States and northern Mexico. Anything worthwhile will take some time and work.

Good money habits are about consistent, healthy actions. When we perform the same consistent actions, we form habits and those actions become automatic. I love automation; no more thinking.

As a child, I loved jumping on the seesaw with someone else. We took turns going up and down as we pushed our feet against the sand when they hit the ground. After reading Franklin's quote on habits, a picture of that childhood seesaw came to mind. On one side of the seesaw were the words "good money habits"; on the other, "bad money habits." In the middle, I saw a pink piggy bank. The amount of money in my pink ceramic friend is directly tied to the stronger money habits. When my good money habits outweigh my bad ones, I have more moolah in the pig than when my bad money habits outweigh my good ones.

The money you currently have is the result of your past behaviors. If you want more money, you need to perform the actions that lead to it. People who amass money perform certain actions and have behaviors that create a result of money accumulation.

Your habits are the key to success with money. You may never get rid of your bad money habits, but that's okay. You don't need to eliminate all the bad habits. Establish better good habits to reduce the negative effects of your bad ones.

Bad money habits include:

- Carrying a credit card balance
- Spending more than you make
- Saving too little

Strengthen your good money habits. Good money habits include:

- Paying yourself first
- Spending less than you earn
- Saving for a rainy day
- Increasing the return you receive on business expenses

As your good money habits become stronger, they will outweigh your bad ones. Inch by inch, anything is a cinch. Let's face it, the chances of any of us will get a huge payday today or tomorrow is next to zero. Yet if we establish the right money habits today, we will all have a significant amount of money ten years from now.

DO A FEW THINGS REALLY WELL

Have you ever tried to use a budget to manage your business? I have. I'll be the first to tell you that budgets are tedious to create and maintain. When people want to get better with money, the first thought many have is, *I need a budget.* I've spent many hours over my career helping businesses create and maintain their budgets. Most people will not abide by a budget because it requires too much work.

Instead, they look at their bank accounts to see how much is there. If there is "enough," then they spend the money. Very few people will take the time to look at their budget to determine if they can "afford" to spend the money. It's too much work.

A CNBC article, "Consumers Overspend By $7,400 A Year," stated that 74% of consumers say they have a budget and 79% of them fail to stick to it.[6] If a budget is a successful money management tool, why don't more people who use it achieve success? Shouldn't the good old reliable budget keep people from overspending? For the vast majority of people, budgets are a losing proposition. I won't teach you to set up a budget. Why waste time on something that doesn't work? I want you use tools that increase your success. For most people, budgets are the New Year's resolutions of improving their money situation. People will stick to a budget for a few weeks and when life happens, as it always does, they will revert to their old patterns of spending.

You don't need to perform Herculean actions to turn your money situation around. Reflect on your rookie year in real estate. Success or failure hinged on you talking with people who wanted to buy or sell a home. You may have been overwhelmed at first, but you learned how to lead-generate through consistent action. As you gained experience, it became easier. Now you have systems that tell you how many people you need to talk to each day to meet your sales goals.

Much like sales, money is a numbers game. When you have the right numbers, you will reach your goals. The amount you currently have in your bank account is the result of your past and current habits. If you want more, establish better money habits. If you have bad money habits now, more money will

---

[6] Sarah O'Brien, "Consumers overspend by $7400 a year. Here are the weekly splurges that cause the most trouble," CNBC, December 26, 2019, https://www.cnbc.com/2019/12/26/consumers-overspend-by-7400-a-year-here-are-weekly-trouble-spots.html.

not improve your money situation. It will make things worse. You'll stay subject to the human problem and spend what you make. Then you will feel worse because of squandered opportunity.

SUCCESS IS GROUNDED IN BOREDOM

You may think that habits are boring. I agree, habits can be boring. If you want to be successful at anything in life, though, be prepared to slog along the path of boredom. Success requires repetition. If you want to sell a lot of homes, you or someone on your team will need to talk to lots of people. It doesn't matter how much you enjoy something; if you do it over and over again, at some point it will become boring. I love chocolate chip cookies. If they were all I ate, I would soon become bored with them and might arrive at a point where the thought of them induced a gag reflex. This reminds me of my college days when many of my meals consisted of peanut butter and jelly on toasted bread. To add some variety, I would switch over to tuna fish sandwiches. Back then, I loved both; but whenever I think of either sandwich now, my stomach begins to turn.

Persistence leads to success. We need to stick with something long enough to see the results of our efforts. Thomas Edison said, "Many of life's failures are people who did not realize how close they were to success when they gave up."[7]

The reason successful people succeed where unsuccessful people fail is they persist when their pursuit becomes boring. They recognize that mastery only comes through repetition. No matter what you do, if you do it long enough, it will become

---

[7] Deborah Hedstrom-Page, *From Telegraph to Light Bulb with Thomas Edison* (Nashville, TN: B&H Publications, 2007).

boring. But you persist because it is important to proceed until you accomplish your objective.

I've completed seven marathons. There were many days when I ran myself into boredom during training. However, I kept running so my body would become accustomed to those additional miles. There is only one way to finish a marathon: Put one foot in front of the other for 26.2 miles. What if I completed twenty-five miles and then decided to quit with the finish line just another mile down the road? Would I get the finisher's medal for completing twenty-five miles? Of course not. When I commit to something, I need to do everything in my power to cross the finish line. If I fail to finish, I am the only one to blame; I didn't do what it took to cross the finish line.

Have you ever run into one of those syrupy, optimistic people whose outlook has no basis in reality? These are the people who think their idea will make them a million dollars during their first month in business, that all they have to do is hang up a shingle and crowds of people will flock to them. I've been that person from time to time. It's easy to get caught up in the optimism of entrepreneurship. No longer do you have a ceiling on your earnings. You have limitless potential. You can create a legacy. Those first days of entrepreneurship are so exciting. The thrill of a new business can't be beat. It's kind of like the skip you feel in your heartbeat when you fall in love. Endorphins course through your veins. The world is a new and better place. The world is your oyster. Nothing can go wrong.

Reality sets in and you realize that, just as in a good relationship, your business needs you to work on it. Everything is rosy until it isn't. If we want a business to fulfill our dreams, we must give it our heart. Nothing more, nothing less.

Henry David Thoreau said, "If you have built castles in the air, your work need not be lost; that is where they should be. Now put the foundations under them."[8]

Be optimistic about your business, but not unrealistic. You'll see good times and bad times. Sometimes the only thing we hold onto in challenging times is hope for something better tomorrow. I'm sure you've had those days when everything seemed to go wrong. During those dark days, find something that inspires you to take one more step—then another step, and another, until you remove yourself from the quagmire of your problems.

THE ROOT CAUSE OF BUSINESS FAILURE

Why do so many real estate agents leave the business? They run out of money. If they made enough money, they would stay in the real estate game.

If money is the root cause of business failure, then profit is the single most important indicator of success. It's time to get real. Your sole purpose for why you work so hard day in and day out is to make money. If you don't have enough money in your bank account, something isn't working. Something is fundamentally broken in your business.

The only way to become rich is to save money. What does saving look like? Spending less than you earn. When I was a child, my favorite activity was opening my piggy bank and counting the bills and coins I had collected. I took great delight in it. I stacked all my coins based on type. I put quarters on top of other quarters, dimes on top of dimes, and Susan B. Anthony coins on top of other Susan B. Anthony coins. I saved

---

[8] Henry David Thoreau, *Walden* (London, England: Macmillan Collector's Library, 2016).

my favorites, the fifty-cent coins, for the last stack. I loved the picture of President Kennedy in profile.

Then I tallied all the bills and coins to find out how much was in my piggy bank. Later, when I was in the army, I highlighted my bank and credit card statements with five different colors so I knew how much money I was spending. Those were my first experiences with counting my money. When I think back on my piggy bank days now, I can't help but smile.

Let's turn back to my dear friend Benjamin Franklin and review his wise words. "Your net worth to the world is usually determined by what remains after your bad habits are subtracted from your good ones."[9]

Omar, a real estate agent in Arizona, had a tremendous track record. He'd been in business for seven years and received the top producer award for the last five. We had our first meeting via internet video.

"Omar, it's exciting to hear about everything you've done so far in your real estate career. What do you need help with?"

"I did $750,000 in commissions last year. I had double-digit growth the last four years and started to build out my team. We continued to get more transactions each year, but I didn't have enough to fund the growth, so I took out a business loan. I thought if I could grow large enough and get the right people in place, my money problems would be solved."

"Tell me more."

"I'm still on a hamster wheel," Omar sighed. "I love helping my agents grow and I'm excited to see their success. However, I look at my bank account and I don't know where all the money went. I am such a hypocrite. Money is always tight. I want to throw in the towel."

_____

[9] Benjamin Franklin Quotes," BrainyQuote.com, accessed October 16, 2021, https://www.brainyquote.com/quotes/benjamin_franklin_151624.

"How much did you pay yourself last month?" I asked.

"Good question."

"How much does it cost you to run your business each month?"

"I wish I knew."

"Got it. I reviewed your numbers, and last year, 80% of your commissions were spent on business expenses. Your tax bill ate up another 15% of your commissions, which only left 5% for you."

"Wow. No wonder I feel so deprived. How do we fix this?"

"What I find is that most businesses struggle because their business expenses gobble up too much of the income. We need to adjust your business spending so you get the most bang for your buck."

Omar smiled. "That sounds good. It means I'll have more without having to sell additional houses."

"That's correct. The habit you need to establish is saving money."

He frowned and replied, "That sounds boring."

"So what if it's boring? If it works, does it matter if it's boring?"

"I guess not. My way hasn't worked. I will try it your way."

It's time for you to start with your first small step—save money. Pick a dollar amount you can save every month. My initial recommendation is for you to save 1% of your income. If you can afford to live on 100% of your income, you can live on 99% of your income. You will quickly discover that you live just as well on 99%. Over time, your savings account will grow. You will develop a sense of pride and security that comes from cash in the bank.

If 1% of your income appears to be too much, then pick a dollar amount. It could be one hundred dollars, fifty dollars, ten dollars, or just one dollar. You can easily save twenty dollars. Most people spend more than twenty dollars when they go out to eat. The most important thing to establish a habit is to start. When you take good actions, you will receive good results. Good habits automate good actions. Have you ever heard anyone claim that they regretted saving money? I haven't. Once you establish a savings habit, keep saving some amount of money for the rest of your life. Saving should be like breathing. Only stop if you want to expire.

KNOWLEDGE IS NOT ENOUGH

All the knowledge in the world is useless unless you act. Success with money is never a one-time event. It is a continuous, everyday process, just like taking care of your health. You need the right habits in place to reap the rewards of good financial actions. If you want healthy finances, you must practice healthy financial actions. The best way to practice healthy financial actions is to establish the right money habits. Then you can put those actions on autopilot.

Money abides by the law of actions and results. If you take bad money actions, do you think you will get desirable results? No. Of course not. If you spend more money than you make, will you have surplus cash? No. You cannot experience good money results from bad money actions. You will always reap what you sow. Your money actions are the tangible representation that you believe your knowledge is correct. If you don't have enough faith to act, your knowledge will not serve you.

Your money actions will always take the path of least resistance if you let them. If you ever questioned why you don't have money at the end of the month, it is because you spent it. Money buys convenience. Going to a fast-food restaurant is more convenient than shopping at the grocery store and cooking. Every action has a result. When we plant a tomato seed, a tomato plant grows. Wouldn't it be weird if an oak tree grew from a tomato seed? Be intentional with the money seeds you plant. You will always reap what you sow.

You cannot spend more than you make and expect to get ahead. You can't neglect to save money for a rainy day and expect money to magically appear when the raindrops do.

GO SMALL TO GO BIG

The present is the best time to improve your future. You can't live your life thinking that your finances will suddenly fix themselves on their own. Your finances are inanimate objects. They will do whatever job you give them. If you don't have your desired amount of cash in the bank, now is the time to act.

The direction you are heading in is more important than the speed at which you travel.

Don't wait until tomorrow. Begin saving today.

Everything starts with a seed. What seed will you plant? Do you want to be rich? Put money into a savings account now.

You don't have to start with a lot. Can you save a dollar? Start with a dollar. Then, next month, save two dollars. You are worth it. You don't need to do a lot. You just need to do one thing now. Start saving money now. Set up a savings account and start saving every time you get paid.

Plug the leaks in your bank account. A part of everything you earn is yours to keep. You worked hard for it. Quit giving everything you earn to the grocery store, the clothes factory, the fast-food restaurants, and all the purveyors of stuff. You have enough stuff. Give yourself the gift of collecting money instead of stuff. See how your life changes when you preserve some of your money for you instead of for stuff. Clink. Clink. Listen to the sound as you make deposits into your piggy bank.

Bill Gates, cofounder of Microsoft, was meticulous about the cash he had in his bank accounts. When he hired people, he believed he took on a mantle of responsibility for them and their families. In the early days of his business, he constantly looked at his bank accounts. He scribbled numbers on a napkin. He performed calculations. He wanted to know if he had enough money. What would happen if his customers didn't pay him for an entire year? He wanted to make sure he had enough to pay all of his employees for twelve months no matter what.

Wow, what a concept. For much of my life, Gates has been the richest man in the world. How would your life be different if you had enough cash in the bank to weather a yearlong storm during which nobody paid you? Does it surprise you that Bill Gates became the richest person in the world? What can you do to build a war chest of cash? How would a ton of cash protect you?

Small savings today lead to a war chest of cash tomorrow.

CHAPTER 3:

DETERMINE WHERE YOU STAND

The first step to success with money is to understand your current money situation. It is next to impossible to chart a course to your destination if you don't know your starting point.

A few years ago, I went on a backpacking trip. It fascinates me to pack everything I need to live in a backpack. One of the things I enjoy most is not knowing what I will encounter on my trip. It's a grand adventure—something new.

I invited a few people to join me, but everyone who committed bailed at the last moment. I looked forward to my time in the forest for several weeks. I planned everything I believed necessary to have a safe trip. I had my compass, map, and cell phone in case of emergencies.

The trailhead I chose is near the summit of Mount Mitchell, the highest peak in the US east of the Mississippi. The Blue Ridge Mountains are a sight to behold. After I took a few pictures at the top of the mountain to memorialize the start of my terrific trek, I found the trailhead and began to hike down the mountain.

About forty-five minutes later, the trail came to a paved road. I looked across the asphalt for the two-inch white circles, emblazoned on trees, that had so far indicated the trail. The last thing I wanted was to get lost in the woods.

Where is the trail marker?

I walked along the paved road and searched for a white dot. I couldn't find one. After ten minutes, I found myself at a fork in the road. I saw a big brown sign with white lettering that marked the entrance of Mount Mitchell State Park. I had passed it when I drove to the parking lot at the top of Mount Mitchell an hour before.

At least I knew where I was. The problem was, I couldn't figure out where I was on my map. I pulled out my compass. I could easily see which way was north. I stared at the map for a few minutes. I frowned. I still couldn't determine my location on the map. I looked up at the ridgeline. I reexamined the map and decided to turn right. It appeared to be the correct way.

Hey, it must be right to turn right.

With thirty-five pounds on my back, a few drops of rain wandered across my bald head. Sixty seconds later, the clouds let forth their fury in a torrential downpour. Fortunately, I had brought my red rain jacket. I quickly put it on. I also pulled out my orange backpack cover and covered the olive-green backpack to keep my food, clothing, tent and sleeping bag dry.

I hiked on in the rain. Every mile or two, I stopped to get my bearings. I told myself I was headed in the right direction. I tried to pull out my cell phone to get my GPS working. No luck. Cell network signals often bounce around the mountains, and it is hard to pick up a stable signal. After about five miles, I concluded that I wasn't headed in the right direction. I turned around.

I found myself back in front of the brown Mount Mitchell State Park sign. *What should I do?* Turning right hadn't worked, so left must be the correct way to go. I walked another five miles and went nowhere fast; still no trail markers to be found. I looked at my watch and realized that I had about two hours before sunset. The rain had stopped and it was time to quit for the day. I set up my tent and called a relative who lived nearby. I asked her to pick me up at the state park sign in the morning so I could get back to my car and drive home. Then I saw another hiker coming toward me.

"Excuse me," I called to him. "Are you familiar with this area?"

"Yes, I hike here all the time."

"I'm hiking the Mountains to Sea Trail, and I started at the top of Mount Mitchell. I was doing well and then all of a sudden, I couldn't find the trail markers and I got lost."

"That's a common problem. The Mountains to Sea Trail isn't marked very well up here."

"I wish I'd known that when I started a few hours ago," I said, but he had already walked past me without volunteering any further information.

I felt defeated. When I returned home, I reviewed the trail guide, which included hiking directions and prominent landmarks. I discovered that there were two trailheads at the top of Mount Mitchell: one for the eastbound trail and the other for the westbound trail. I had taken the westbound trail. *If only I had brought the trail guide with me, I wouldn't have gotten lost.* No wonder I couldn't figure out where I was on the map. The entire time, I had lugged my heavy olive-green backpack on the wrong trail. All the preparation and planning were for naught because I wasn't on the right path.

You don't have to go it alone anymore. There is a clear path to business prosperity. I'll be your guide, so you don't have to wander around lost without knowing it like I did that day in the mountains of North Carolina.

In this chapter, we'll start with the foundation of your finances. I'll show you how to calculate the most important financial number you need to know. Almost every real estate agent I talk to knows their annual commission income goal. However, when I ask many of them how much they need or want to support their personal lifestyle, all I get is a blank stare and a muffled "I don't know." It is difficult to build a business that supports your lifestyle if you don't know how much you want to spend on it. I call this amount your Personal Lifestyle Number. This is the amount of money you spend to live your life. Without this critical piece of data, you run the risk of trotting along at a fast clip westward when you want to go east. You'll huff and puff and put in all the long hours only to end up tired and unclear about what your next step should be.

PERSONAL LIFESTYLE NUMBER

The very first thing I ask a new client is, "How much do you spend each month to support your lifestyle?" Very few people have a direct answer for this question. A year before I began writing this book, I was in the same boat. I had an inkling of what it cost to cover all my bills, but I didn't know for sure. I didn't take the time to review my bank and credit card statements each month. Why? It was too tedious to track personal spending. I needed a simple system that would run on autopilot.

I had tried many systems before, but none of them stuck. Either they were too tedious or took too much time. I needed a system that served me, not one I served. It needed to make my life simpler and easier. I didn't want something too complicated that I needed to "fit" into my already overcrowded life. I knew it was critical to have a system to inform me if I spent more than I made each month. My happiness depended on me being responsible with my money.

In his book *David Copperfield*, Charles Dickens wrote, "Annual income twenty pounds, annual expenditure nineteen [pounds] nineteen [shillings] and six [pence], result happiness. Annual income twenty pounds, annual expenditure twenty pounds ought and six, result misery."[10]

I'll translate this for us in the modern-day world. If you make $50,000 a year and spend $49,995, you will be happy. If you earn $50,000 and spend $50,005, you will be miserable. Spend five dollars less than you make and all is right with the world. Spend five dollars more than you make and you are in for a world of hurt, as if you just got sucker punched by a prize-winning boxer.

First, you must know how much you spend. This is your Personal Lifestyle Number. What's included in it? Everything you spend money on. If you're like most people, you don't know how much you spend each month. You may have a hunch, but unless you look at your finances on regular basis, the hunch may be incorrect. It may be a larger number than you realize.

Everyone knows they should keep track of their finances, yet few people do. Most people think it is a pain in the neck to stay in tune with their personal finances. They think they need a fancy computer software program. They think they need to track their bills and spending in a spreadsheet. While I love spreadsheets, many real estate agents I talk with would rather have their brains scooped out with a soup ladle than look at a spreadsheet.

While finance software and spreadsheets are useful, many don't use them because they are too much work for the average person. You've got clients to serve, food to put on the table, garages to clean out, groceries to buy, lawns to mow, soccer games to attend, etc. If you had a choice between a root canal and tracking your money, you might be the first in line for the root canal. Doctor, please drill away to your heart's content.

---

[10] Charles Dickens, *David Copperfield* (New York, NY: Modern Library, 2000).

Bzzz. Most of these tasks, including dealing with the cluttered garage with no room for your car, are more exciting than tracking finances.

Most people manage their finances by what Mike Michalowicz, in his book *Profit First*, calls bank balance accounting.[11] When they want to buy something, they look at their bank account. If there's money in it, they spend it. It there isn't enough, they abstain. Then there are the people who throw caution to the wind and spend, spend, spend without looking to see if there is enough. They pull out the credit card and charge as if they were army generals taking on the enemy.

It is natural for us to spend what we make. We're used to our success in earning money and tend to treat it as a natural phenomenon, similar to the way we expect the sun to rise in the east at the dawn of each new day. The idea that it might not rise is inconceivable to us. We fall prey to this tendency with our money. Money replenishes itself each month, so why not spend everything we make? After all, we can't take it with us.

When we spend everything we make, we give control of our money to others. We live our lives as rudderless ships in the middle of the sea. We even build raccoon houses next to our beds so that Clyde, The Human Problem, can fill our dreams with all the wonderful things we might spend our money on. When the sun shines brightly, all appears well. However, when the storms come—as they always do—we are helpless in the winds and waves. You owe it to yourself to pay yourself first, so you have a steady rudder to keep your business headed in the direction you determine. Let's redirect your inner army general

---

[11] Mike Michalowicz, *Profit First: Transform Your Business from a Cash-Eating Monster to a Money-Making Machine* (New York, NY: Portfolio | Penguin Publishing Group, 2017).

toward building awareness of your spending, so you have a healthy financial future. You deserve it.

You may have heard that many lottery winners are broke within five years after they strike it rich. They may have struggled for years, even decades, to eke out a living and keep food on the table. All the while, they've heard about America the Beautiful, where dreams come true. When they finally hit the big one, all those crisp dollar bills slip through their fingers like a handful of sand from the beach.

While circumstances change from time to time, unless we change our behaviors around money, we will always revert to what we are comfortable with. It's human nature. We love to reside in our comfort zones. After all, there is a reason they call it a comfort zone—because it's comfortable.

PERSONAL EXPENSE CALCULATOR

I developed the Personal Expense Calculator to give me a simple, quick method to generate my Personal Lifestyle Number—how much I spend in my personal life. I once was the proverbial cobbler whose children wore no shoes. I knew how to help others with their finances, but I had zero clarity about my own. Day in and day out, I looked at other people's finances. The last thing I wanted to do with my time off was spend it looking at more numbers.

But I also knew that I needed to heed Charles Dickens's advice. Unless I knew how much I spent and earned, I would remain clueless about my financial picture. A consequence of this cluelessness was anxiety. When I thought about money, my heart pounded with worry and blood raced through my veins as if trying to win the Kentucky Derby. If I allowed myself to ruminate on it too much, I'd enter a spiral of overthinking and confusion. When it became too overwhelming, I'd stuff all those thoughts and feelings under my bed for another day when, hopefully, the problems would resolve themselves.

Much to my dismay, things didn't work themselves out. They only got worse. I had to face reality: If I didn't know how much I spent or earned, how could I determine if I was getting ahead or digging myself into a pit? I needed objective data instead of a hunch. Once I knew my Personal Lifestyle Number, I would be crystal clear about how much money my business needed to make to keep the lights on and food in my four children's bellies.

Can you imagine trying to sell fifty homes this year without a clear system to track how many houses you've sold so far? How would you know if you needed to step up your game to get more homes under contract? If it makes sense to track the progress of your sales goals, doesn't it make sense to keep the pulse of how much you spend and earn?

With the Personal Expense Calculator, all you need is a blank piece of paper, a pen and the last three months of your personal bank and credit card statements. For example, if you are reading this in June, you need the statements for March, April, and May. The best thing about this method is, you can complete it in a few minutes. There are less than ten steps. And once you've completed it, you will know how much you earn and spend each month.

On your piece of paper, create a table like Table 1. (After you fill it in, it will look something like Table 2.)

Before you fill in the cells, determine which of the following credit card-user types you are:

- **Nonuser**—you don't use credit cards
- **Full Payer**—you pay off your credit card balance each month
- **Revolver**—you carry a balance

TABLE 1: PERSONAL EXPENSE CALCULATOR					
	Month 1	Month 2	Month 3	Total	Average
Spending					

TABLE 2: PERSONAL EXPENSE CALCULATOR EXAMPLE					
	Month 1	Month 2	Month 3	Total	Average
Spending	7,000	6,000	8,000	21,000	7,000

If you are a revolver, you will perform an extra step that is detailed in the Revolver Steps section. If you are a nonuser or a full payer, that step isn't applicable to you; you will only need the last three months of your personal bank statements to complete the table.

Look at the summary pages of your bank statements. They show your beginning balance, deposits, checks cashed, payments made, and ending balance for each month. You will use this information to complete the table.

Here are the steps to use the Personal Expense Calculator:

1. Look at the total spending on your Month 1 bank statement. You might see one number for total checks and one number for total payments, or these may be split up into a few categories. If you have more than one such number on your bank statement, add them together and write the sum in the Month 1 Spending box. If you only have one number, write it in the Month 1 Spending box.
2. Repeat step 1 for the other two months.
3. Add the three months of spending together and write the amount in the Total box.

4. Divide the total by three and write the amount in the Average box.

5. Look at the amount in the Average box. This is how much money you spend each month.

6. Pat yourself on the back, because you now know your Personal Lifestyle Number.

You have now completed a task few people perform. The vast masses slog through a fog of ambiguity, living paycheck to paycheck. Is it any wonder people worry so much about money? They haven't taken the first step toward figuring out where they stand, so they wander aimlessly, as I did while trekking on Mount Mitchell's westbound trail when my car was parked to the east.

Compare the amount you spend with your income. Which amount is larger? Are you surprised by the numbers? I estimate that most people spend 120% of their monthly income. Very few people see more cash in their bank accounts at the end of each month. They allow Clyde, The Human Problem, to overpower their lives. They spend more than they earn.

THE REVOLVER STEPS

If you are a revolver who carries a credit card balance each month, you will use Table 2 and perform a few extra steps to get a true picture of your spending. Each month you make a payment on your credit card, so we factor it into your spending.

On your piece of paper, create a table like Table 3.

To complete the Revolver Steps Table, you need copies of your last three months of bank and credit card statements.

TABLE 3: REVOLVER STEPS					
	Month 1	Month 2	Month 3	Total	Average
Bank Spending					
Credit Card Purchases					
Credit Card Payments					
Total Spending					

Bank Statement Steps

1. Look at the total spending on your Month 1 bank statement. You might see one number for checks and another for total payments, or these may be split up into a few categories. If you have more than one such number on your bank statement, add them together and write the sum in the Bank Spending box under Month 1. If you only have one number, write it in the Bank Spending box under Month 1.
2. Repeat steps 1 and 2 above for the other two months.
3. Add the three months of spending together and write the amount in the Total box.
4. Divide the total by three and write the amount in the Average box.

Credit Card Statement Steps

To make sure we're both using the same language, I'll define a couple of terms I'll be using in this section.

- Credit card purchases are items you buy with your credit card.

- Credit card payments are payments you make to your credit card to pay down the credit card balance.

1. Look at the total purchases, interest, and fees on your Month 1 credit card statement. Add these three together to get your total Month 1 credit card spending. Write the amount in the Credit Card Purchases box under Month 1.
2. Repeat step 1 for the other two months.
3. Look at the total payments and credits. Add them together to get your total Month 1 credit card payments. Add the three months of payments together and write the amount as a negative number in the Credit Card Payments box under Month 1. This is a negative number, since the payments came from your bank spending.
4. Repeat step 3 for the other two months.
5. Divide the total by three and write the amount in the Average box.
6. For Month 1, add the bank spending, credit card purchases, and credit card payments together and write the number in the Total Spending box under Month 1.
7. Repeat step 6 for the other two months.
8. Divide the total by three and write the amount in the Average box.
9. Pat yourself on the back: You now know your Personal Lifestyle Number.

Credit cards are one of the most valuable tools that Clyde, The Human Problem, uses to get us to spend everything we make. In many cases, he gets people to spend *more* than they

	Month 1	Month 2	Month 3	Total	Average
TABLE 4: REVOLVER STEPS EXAMPLE					
Bank Spending	7,000	6,000	8,000	21,000	7,000
Credit Card Purchases	2,900	1,8000	3,600	8,300	2,767
Credit Card Payments	-500	-500	-500	-1,500	-500
Total Spending	9,400	7,300	11,100	27,800	9,267

make—which is much worse than an empty wallet because it forces us to start the next month in a hole. While we max out our credit cards, Bonnie, The Distractor, sends us more credit card applications in the mail. If you can't pay off your credit card in full today, it's time to change your behavior. Stop spending on your credit card now. Use a debit card for all your expenses instead.

Credit cards charge notoriously high interest rates. If you continue to carry a credit card balance, you will kill your profitability. One of the easiest ways to increase your profits is to eliminate all credit card debt. The average credit card interest rate is around 20%. When you carry a credit card balance, you rob your business of 20% profits on all the credit card purchases.

Maybe you get travel points or cash back rewards. Let's say you get a whopping 2% rewards for your spending. Now your average interest rate is 18% instead of 20%. There's a saying in Las Vegas: "The house always wins." Casinos know that if you play long enough, they will come out ahead. Everything in the casinos is designed to keep you in the casinos.

It's exactly the same with credit card companies. They want you to use your credit card every month, because they know they always win. Someday, when you come up short on money, they'll snag you. It's as if they place a medium rare filet mignon in the middle of a bear trap. The aroma of this meat-eaters' delight wafts around you every time you get close to it. You try to resist, but eventually you venture toward the bear trap and it instantly snaps around your arm.

Credit cards can be destructive. Only use them if you pay off the balances every month. If you can't pay them off now, when will you be able to pay them? Stop using your credit cards now. Use a debit card so that you only spend the money you have.

DO YOU MAKE ENOUGH TO SUPPORT YOUR PERSONAL LIFESTYLE NUMBER?

You've calculated your Personal Lifestyle Number. Now it's time to compare it with your income.

On your piece of paper, create the Personal Lifestyle Number table.

1. Look at the total deposits on your Month 1 bank statement. Write the amount in the Deposits box under Month 1.
2. Repeat step 1 for the other two months.
3. Add the three months of spending together and write the amount in the Total box.
4. Divide the total by three and write the amount in the Average box.
5. Refer to the Personal Expense Calculator Table you completed (Table 1). If you are a revolver, you will use the numbers in the Total Spending row of Table 2 (Personal Expense Calculator Example) and enter those into the Spending row of Table 3 (Revolver

TABLE 5: PERSONAL LIFESTYLE NUMBER					
	Month 1	Month 2	Month 3	Total	Average
Deposits					
Spending					
Surplus/Deficit					

Steps Table). Otherwise, you will use the numbers from the Spending row of Table 1.

6. Repeat step 5 for the other two months.
7. Add the three months of spending together and write the amount in the Total box.
8. Divide the total by three and write the amount in the Average box.
9. Calculate the Surplus/Deficit row by subtracting the Spending row from the Deposits row. If you have a positive number, then you have a surplus. If you get a negative number, you have a deficit.
10. Add the three months of surplus/deficit together and write the amount in the Total box.
11. Divide the total by three and write the amount in the Average box.

Compare the amount you spend with your income. Which amount is larger? Are you surprised by the numbers? I estimate that most people spend 120% of their monthly income. Very few people see more cash in their bank accounts at the end of each month. They allow Clyde, The Human Problem, to overpower their lives. They spend everything they make.

If your surplus/deficit is negative, then it's time to adjust. You will not get ahead if you continue to spend more than you make. Think about what you can do to increase your income and decrease expenses until you make your surplus/deficit a positive number.

If your average surplus/deficit is zero or positive, you spend less than you earn. Congratulations! If you continue to spend less than you earn with your personal finances, you can translate this success to your business.

YOUR STARTING POINT

At the beginning of this chapter, I shared the story of how I got lost in the woods on my Mount Mitchell hike. I was convinced everything was fine until I had to admit to myself that I was lost. Until I figured out where I was, I continued to wander aimlessly, carrying a heavy backpack. I was embarrassed when I learned that all those miles I trekked took me farther and farther away from my destination.

Many of the real estate agents I work with are in a similar situation with their personal finances when they start working with me. Once I take them through the process of learning their Personal Lifestyle Number, they gain clarity about how much their business needs to make to provide them with sufficient pay.

It's time to record the three numbers you worked hard to calculate in this chapter. These mark the starting point for your Profit First journey.

Refer to the average numbers in Table 3 and write them down below. You will use these numbers to build a solid foundation for your business:

1. Write the Average Deposits in the Personal Income space below.

2. Write the Average Spending in the Personal Lifestyle Number space below.
3. Write the Average Surplus/Deficit in the Surplus/Deficit space below.

Personal Income _____

Personal Lifestyle Number _____

Surplus/Deficit _____

CHAPTER 4:

THE MONEY PIE

Your next commission check is right around the corner. Pat yourself on the back. Or maybe you should give yourself a big bear hug. Time to enjoy the fruits of your labor. Once you've finished celebrating, take a few moments to ponder the following questions:

- How will you spend it?
- How much of it belongs to you?
- How much belongs to Uncle Sam?
- How much will you use to run your business?

Many people won't have answers for any of these questions. Some believe that the entire commission check belongs to them because they don't have a money system that serves them.

Profit First is the best system for managing your business finances. With it, you will apply a pay-yourself-first philosophy to your business. Consequently, you will get paid first, you will have money to pay your taxes on time, and you will reduce wasteful spending on unnecessary business expenses. Once you have the system in place, you will discover that money is as easy as pie.

What's your favorite pie? You may prefer mincemeat, apple, or cherry. Reflect on your favorite pie as I share the lesson I learned from shoving the delectable, flaky-crusted dessert into my mouth.

My favorite pie is pecan. I love the combination of buttery pecans and ooey-gooey, sugary filling surrounded by a flaky crust. Give me a piece and I'm surrounded by clouds and winged angels whose halos float over their heads as they sing "Hallelujah!" in harmony. As I feasted on music and pie one day, I learned a valuable lesson about money.

Imagine for a minute that every morning, you receive a pie. Each day, you have just enough pie to last you for that day. When it's gone, it's gone. You can eat it all for breakfast, but then you will go hungry for the remainder of the day.

You could split it into three pieces and have one each at breakfast, lunch, and dinner.

You could cut a slice to share with a friend or family member. You could also put a slice in the freezer for a day when the baker gets sick. If you placed a slice in the freezer daily, you would soon have a whole pie for a rainy day.

Everything goes well until one makes a disastrous decision and eats more than one pie per day. They overindulge; they rob from tomorrow to eat too much today. As they binge, their appetite grows beyond one pie a day. They get used to being stuffed. However, they are only given one pie each day. They eat beyond their means. If they stuck with eating only one pie per day, they would always have enough.

Money works the same way. Every day, we get a money pie. If we don't eat more of our money pie than we receive, we will be fine. We will have enough money.

However, when we eat more than we have, we become indebted to others. Our appetite grows. We travel toward a vicious downward spiral of permanent debt that shackles us and weighs us down. The first step toward gaining control over your money is to live each day on the money pie you have for that day. See, I told you: Money is as easy as pie.

OWNER PAY FIRST

Mike Michalowicz and I sat across from each other at a table in a hotel restaurant. After we caught up, we began to talk about what I planned to write about in this book.

"Mike, I have a bone to pick with you about the title 'Profit First.'"

"Interesting. Tell me more."

"I don't agree that profit should be first. The first goal of a business should be to pay the owner. You can't have a profit if the owner doesn't make enough money to pay themselves."

Mike smiled and said, "Damon, one of the things I've always said is that Profit First is the pay-yourself-first principle applied to business."

"I do remember you told me that on a few occasions."

"Part of the reason I chose 'Profit First' is, I wanted to be edgy. There is some disdain in America about profits. People complain about corporate greed. By titling the book *Profit First*, I planted my flag in the ground. I declared that businesses need to be profitable above all else."

"Philosophically, you and I are on the same page. However, we both have our own twist on it. I'll stick to my guns and say owner pay first."

Mike laughed and said, "I'm glad you're writing your book. People need to hear your viewpoint."

Profit First is a fancy-schmancy title, but I think it should be revamped. Profit is not the first goal of a business. Owner pay comes first. The first goal should be to pay the owner enough to cover their living expenses. (I'm not talking about mansions,

Ferraris and swimming pools full of gold bullion. Wait a second, it would be difficult to swim in said pool. I think I'll stick with good old-fashioned H_2O, thank you.) If you struggle to put food on the table, focusing on profit may not resonate with you. First, make enough to pay yourself.

It's important to prioritize work based on your current needs. You won't solve your most pressing problems if you work on unimportant ones. For example, if your business doesn't have enough sales to pay you, it would be foolish to create an employee handbook. A proper employee handbook will do little to create sales. Your business needs to create and keep enough money to pay for your lifestyle. Until your business rewards you with enough money to support you and your family, you will be caught in a scarcity mindset and worry constantly about where your next home sale will come from.

One of my clients, George, came to my office to meet with me. As we sat across from each other at my toffee-colored conference room table, he spoke about the new hires he had made to expand his real estate team. I listened as he shared his optimism about the new direction of his business, but then his voice grew thin and unsteady as he said, "I'm growing, but I'm still worried. I'm eating into my savings to make ends meet at home."

"That reminds me of where I was two years after I started my CPA firm," I told George. "I was overworked, tired, and out of money. I was bewildered, too, because at the end of the month there wasn't enough money left to pay myself. I made more money in year two than I did my first year. Yet when I looked at my numbers, I realized I had spent more as well. Everyone else was paid more than me. Why should I work so hard to make a pittance? I remember mumbling to myself, 'It's not fair. It's not fair.'"

"What did you do?" asked George.

"I sat in thought for a while. I was tense as I contemplated how to right the ship of my business. If I didn't get paid enough, then what was the point of being in business?

"As I sat with my brow scrunched up tightly, a thought popped into my head. *Damon, you're failing because you're not paying yourself first.* It was a flash of inspiration. I knew instantly that this was the solution to my problem.

"I drove to my bank and set up a new bank account. I nicknamed it the Damon bank account. Then, every time a client paid me, I moved 10% of that payment to my Damon bank account. To this day, it is the best financial decision I ever made. In six short weeks, I had more than $1,500 in my Damon bank account, which was enough to cover my mortgage. While that amount may not sound like a lot to you, back then it was a fortune for me. All that built-up tension in my neck muscles began to melt away. The decision to pay myself first turned my business around. My dread turned into excitement. I knew that if I continued to pay myself first, I wouldn't need to worry about money."

"But in my business, my employees come first," George said.

"Who is the hardest-working employee in your business?"

"I don't know."

"It's you. If something goes wrong, you're responsible. You will stay until the wee hours of the morning to ensure that you deliver for your clients. If you're the most important employee, shouldn't you be paid the most?"

"I never thought of it like that before. I always thought my employees should be paid before me."

You must be paid first, before anyone else in the company. If you don't get paid, you rob yourself and your loved ones. You fall on your sword and sacrifice yourself for those you choose to serve in a life of wailing and suffering. You shouldn't have to suffer needlessly. When you neglect yourself with inadequate pay, you neglect everyone who is important in your life—your clients, your family, your friends, your community. You have a duty to be successful. The first step toward success is to pay yourself first for the value you bring into other people's lives.

If you want to be rich and make millions of dollars a year, I'm all for that. Before you get to the seven-, eight- and nine-figure wealth, though, you must start with one dollar. Start small to go big. Don't diminish your dream. Make sure you build your dream on a solid foundation.

The foundation to success begins with owner pay.

There are a lot of misconceptions about owner pay. Is it an owner's salary? Is it an owner's distributions or draws? Is it those "business trips" to Maui for corporate retreats? Is it the fancy car? My answer to each of these questions is yes. Owner pay is any compensation paid by the company for the owner's benefit.

Items I typically include in owner pay are:

- Salary
- Luxury vehicles
- Owner health insurance
- Company retirement contributions to the owner
- Personal business trips
- Owner distributions
- Any expense run through the business for tax-savings purposes

Some real estate agents drive fancy cars. Cars are the ultimate status symbol you can take with you anywhere you go. Some have spent more on their vehicles than I did on my first townhome. If you want to spend your resources on a luxury, go for it. However, your real estate business doesn't need you to drive a six-figure car. You don't have to drive a beater, either. Drive a clean, well-maintained, and professional car. You don't need a house on wheels to be a successful real estate agent.

If you choose to drive a luxury vehicle, classify it as owner pay. Those four wheels are part of your compensation package. Would it be logical for someone to spend $2,500 a month on their car and not receive a paycheck? What if they complained about not having enough to cover their mortgage payment? They would be better off with a lower car payment so they can keep the lights on.

Much of the confusion around business finance has to do with the fact that people lack clarity about where the money goes. This leads to a condition I call "muddy water," where it's hard to see through the suspended silt. There is just too much visual noise. In order to see clearly, it's important to remove the noise; then the water will be clean. When you have muddy water, you don't know if your business is making or losing money. But when you put clear labels on how you spend money, you gain clarity. You understand what works or doesn't work in the business. Consequently, you know if the business makes enough to pay you.

THE FOUR USES OF MONEY IN YOUR BUSINESS

There are only four ways you will spend money in your business. Four is a lot less to deal with than the fifteen to thirty categories you will typically hear about from bookkeepers and accountants. You may be on top of your game and receive a profit and loss (P&L) statement from your own accountant or bookkeeper. I've worked with hundreds of real estate agents, and many of them don't understand how to read a P&L statement.

You are in Chapter 4 of this book, and I'm just now bringing up the P&L statement. Many will tell you it is the key to understanding your business finances. While it can be important, it misleads most real estate agents who try to use it. I prioritized this book based on what is most important for you to get ahead with your money, so I'll leave all further discussion of P&L statements to Chapter 10. There are more important things for you to focus on to achieve success with your money than having an up-to-date P&L statement.

Remember, in Chapter 1, I stated that the two golden keys of money are:

- **Pay yourself first.**
- **Spend less than you earn.**

I also shared that money is more about your behavior than it is about numbers. In this chapter, you'll get two frameworks that will help you build the proper habits to win with money.

Your business must spend less than it earns each month. If it doesn't, you will fall behind and dig yourself into a hole. With the money pie in your business, you split all your income into four slices: owner pay, profit, tax, and business expenses. Every dollar from every commission you earn from now on needs to be split properly between the four slices. Anytime you spend money, it will be in one of these four areas. Remember, money is easy as pie. Don't overthink this. Don't overcomplicate this.

The Money Pie

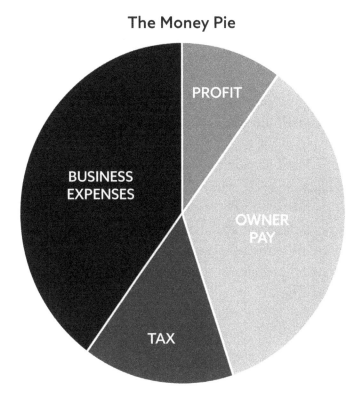

There are only four uses of money in your business:

Owner Pay: This is what you, as the owner, receive in the form of a salary and other benefits.

Profit: This is the extra money your business receives for the work it does.

Tax: This is payment for all the foundational work the government does to make the free enterprise system available to you as a business owner.

Business Expenses: These are payments to your vendors and employees for the work and supplies they provide to support you and your clients.

That's it. Four uses of money in your businesses.

Everyone deserves to be paid fairly. We could argue about how much one person should or should not get paid, but it would serve no purpose. If you've complained about how much you pay your employees, vendors, or in taxes, pause for a moment and ask yourself this question: Am I paid fairly?

If the answer is no, ask another question: "What needs to change so I will be paid fairly from now on?" It's your money pie; you deserve to be paid for your value. When everyone gets paid appropriately, everyone wins.

Money will vacate your business unless you have a system with guardrails around spending. Every dollar of your business must have a predetermined purpose when you receive it. Otherwise, you might as well douse your wads of cash with some gasoline, light a match and start a bonfire. What a waste. When there are so many good things you can do with your money, don't fall victim to inertia.

Here is the flawed formula by which most people run their businesses:

$$SALES - EXPENSES = PROFIT$$

The problem with this formula is, it emphasizes the wrong things. The order in which we do things matters. The most important element of the above equation, profit, comes last. Usually, the last thing gets the least attention.

Think about sitting down for dinner. You look down at your plate and see a juicy steak, mashed potatoes, and some broccoli. If you eat the steak and the potatoes before you eat the broccoli, the pile of small green trees will remain on your plate when your belly is full. However, if you eat the broccoli first, you will consume all three portions of your meal and get the wonderful nutrients from your broccoli.

Here is the Profit First formula Mike Michalowicz introduced in his book *Profit First*:[12]

SALES – PROFIT = EXPENSES

When we change the formula, we change our focus.

As powerful as Mike's Profit First formula is, it doesn't include all the vital information we need to have a holistic view of our businesses.

Here is the Profit First for Real Estate Agents formula:

SALES – PROFIT – OWNER PAY – TAX = EXPENSES

Notice how owner pay is in the middle of the Profit First for Real Estate Agents formula. It is the most important number in the entire formula. It is similar to your heart, beating rhythmically in the middle of your rib cage. If you are not adequately paid for the blood, sweat, tears, energy, sleepless nights, ball-juggling, pounding your head against the wall, and pushing outside of your comfort zones, you will eventually resent the business. If you invest everything you have in your business, you need to be richly rewarded for your pound of flesh.

THE DREAM HOME BUSINESS

You're in the dream home business. Your primary objective is to help your clients find a home they will love at a price they can afford. I want you to think a bit differently about the words "dream home business." Think about what the word "home" means to your clients. What does home mean to you? Truly, there is no place like home. What if your business was your dream home, one where you love to reside and where you build

---

[12] Michalowicz, *Profit First*.

your happiest memories? I want you to have your Dream Home Business.

We will use the concepts from the money pie to build your Dream Home Business.

Imagine a house with a foundation, two floors, and a roof—four levels to match the four slices of the money pie.

The first thing you need in a house is a solid foundation. In your business, the first thing you need to cover is owner pay. Nobody in the business should be paid before the owner. Consequently, you will build your business to first pay you as the owner. Owner pay is the foundation of your Dream Home Business.

Once your business earns enough to cover your Personal Lifestyle Number, you want to build the first floor: profit. When you have profit in your business, you have more money in your bank account at the end of the month than you had at the beginning. The purpose of your business should be to create surplus cash.

The second floor is tax. Yes, tax. Taxes are part of business life.

One of my clients, Ginny, called me on the phone and said, "Damon, I hate paying taxes."

"Tell me more."

"It's just so much money," she groaned.

"I would love for you to pay a million dollars in taxes."

I could hear Ginny's bewilderment in the silent pause that ensued. Then she said, somewhat ironically, "If I paid a million in taxes, it would mean I made a lot of money."

"Exactly. Paying lots of taxes is a sign of success."

I want you to be successful—which means you'll pay a lot of taxes. While you shouldn't pay more than your fair share, it's important to have tax money set aside so you can pay your tax bill when it's due.

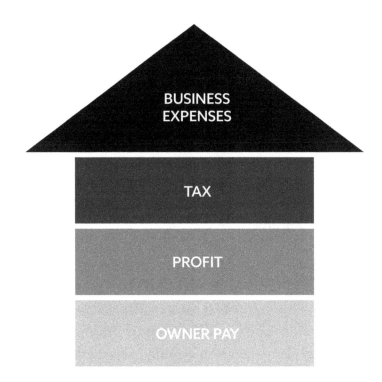

Once you have a two-story house, complete with owner pay, profit, and tax, it's time to add the roof. Business expenses are the roof of your Dream Home Business. You want enough of a roof to protect the foundation and two floors. No more, no less. Think about this the next time you sell a home. How many of your clients come to you and rave about the roof of their dream home? Probably not even one. But just like the roof of a house, your business expenses keep everything below in good shape.

What would happen if the roof you placed on a house was too heavy? The house would groan and creak from the strain. The excess weight would eventually cause cracks to form in the walls and, left untreated, the house could suffer catastrophe. The same thing happens when business expenses are too much for your Dream Home Business. When real estate agents run into problems with their money, it is usually because of roofs that are too heavy.

If you build it properly, your Dream Home Business will protect you from The Devious Duo. They will be stuck outside, yelling "Let me in!" like the Big Bad Wolf as you recline on your sofa next to the fire, roasting marshmallows for an evening treat of s'mores. Bonnie, The Distractor, will have no sway because you're focused on growing cash in the bank. Clyde, The Human Problem, will be powerless against you because you split your money pie up properly.

THE PROFIT FIRST BANK ACCOUNTS

When you give money a job, it has a greater chance of success. Life gets busy with the day to day, and many people don't spend time front-end planning how they want to spend their money. This leads to money flowing out of their bank accounts. If you don't plan how you will spend your money, Bonnie and Clyde will rob you.

Remember the two fundamental principles of money:

- **Pay yourself first.**
- **Spend less than you earn.**

If you obey these two fundamental principles, you will be in control of your money. Be diligent with your money. Show it you are the boss. When you establish a predetermined purpose for your money, you tell it how it will be spent. At the same time, you tell it how it will *not* be spent.

The best way to separate the slices of your money pie is with the use of several bank accounts. Most likely, you've used more than one bank account before. If you've had a checking account and a savings account, you know how this works. If you've put money into a retirement account, you've directed your money where you want it to go.

The Profit First bank accounts are the most effective way to properly separate your money and relegate it to owner pay, profit, tax, and business expenses. Set up the following five main bank accounts for your Profit First system:

- **Income**
- **Profit**
- **Owner Pay**
- **Tax**
- **Business Expenses**

The **Income** bank account is where you deposit all your commission checks and deposits. It is used as a holding account until it's time to transfer the money to the other four accounts. The only time you move money out of the **Income** account is when you do your Profit First bank transfers. When you do your Profit First bank transfers, you will empty your **Income** account and split the money between the other four bank accounts on a pro rata basis. In Chapter 6, I'll provide you with more guidance on when to move the money to the other accounts.

The **Owner Pay** bank account is used to pay you as an employee of the business. You perform work for the business and are an employee. Make sure you pay yourself a fair wage. If you hired someone else to perform your job, what would you pay them?

The **Profit** account is where you collect your profit—the money your business receives for its success. If you have no profit, your business is not currently successful. Remember, profit equals cash in the bank. If there is no cash in the bank, your business is not profitable.

The **Tax** account is to pay your taxes. Benjamin Franklin said, "In this world nothing can be said to be certain, except death and taxes!"[13] If you don't pay your taxes, you will feel like death warmed over.

The **Business Expenses** account is used to pay vendors and employees. This account puts boundaries around your spending. The money you deposit into the **Business Expenses** account is the only source of funds you have to spend on running your business.

You may wonder, "How do I choose a bank that will work for my real estate business?" When you set up your Profit First for Real Estate Agents bank accounts, look for the following:

- Minimal or no banking fees.
- Low minimum balances.

When I say low, a $100 minimum balance is what I look for as ideal. You get bonus points if you can open accounts with zero-dollar minimums.

Consider the features and benefits you get with the bank. Remember, you get what you pay for. Sometimes trying to get something for free isn't worth it.

If you have a good banking relationship already, tell your banker you want to add a few new bank accounts. Explain the reasons for the additional accounts. If you're so inclined, send me your banker's information and I'll send them a free copy of *Profit First for Real Estate Agents*.

If your current bank charges minimum fees, you can always ask that they be waived. Tell your banker that the additional bank accounts will help you grow your cash reserves. If your banker won't waive the fees, decide if it still makes sense to stay with them or if you want to look for a new bank.

---

[13] Walter Isaacson, *Benjamin Franklin: An American Life* (New York, NY: Simon & Schuster, 2003).

FIND A NEW BANK

Work with a local community bank. I love the two I use. I have a personal relationship with bankers at both banks. If you have plans to grow your business, you may need a loan. The best and least expensive source of funds will probably be with a local bank. Part of their banking charter is to lend in the local community. Typically, lending decisions are made at the branch level. The alternative is to work with a large national bank where those decisions are made at national headquarters, far away from you. It may be a royal pain to switch to or away from this kind of bank.

If you go to the branch office to set up your bank accounts, it will take a couple hours. This may seem like a lot of time to take out of your day. However, it will be worth the effort. Once the bank accounts are set up, you'll have everything you need to take care of the money side of your business.

Here is a hack to save you time when set up your accounts: Call your banker and explain the accounts you want to open and have them notify you once they are set up. You will need to sign some paperwork. When your banker sets up the accounts before you come in, it may take fifteen to thirty minutes at most to sign the paperwork. Then you'll be good to go.

OUT OF SIGHT, OUT OF MIND MONEY

Think about a traditional retirement account. When you contribute to an account like this, you set it and forget it. For example, if you put 5% of your paycheck into a retirement account, you won't miss it because you didn't have a chance to spend it. You'll adjust your spending to what's left over.

Profit and tax are two slices of your money pie that you will access only once per quarter. Consequently, they are best kept less accessible so you don't spend them on something else. To put the out of sight, out of mind principle into place, you will set up two savings accounts at a separate bank which we will call bank two. Bank one is where you set up your **Income**, **Owner Pay**, and **Business Expenses** checking accounts. When you do your bank transfers, you will move your profit and tax money to the savings accounts at bank two. With the money in separate bank accounts, you will forget it is there. Then, at the end of each quarter, you will issue yourself a profit bonus check and pay your quarterly tax payments.

Here are the results you will experience once you have your new, Profit First for Real Estate Agents bank accounts set up:

- Your business will be permanently profitable.
- You will be guaranteed a paycheck that covers your personal lifestyle and expenses.
- You won't have to worry about paying a tax bill because you will have money set aside for it.
- You will establish limits for business expenses.
- You will have clarity on where and how much you spend.

Wayne Dyer said, "If you change the way you look at things, the things you look at change."[14]

With the Profit First system, you change the way you look at your business finances in a powerful and meaningful way. You make profit a vital part of your business, not an afterthought.

SET UP YOUR ACCOUNTS

You're a smart business owner and you've already set up your bank accounts, right? You've got the following three checking

---

[14] Wayne Dyer, *Everyday Wisdom for Success* (Carlsbad, CA: Hay House, 2006).

accounts at your primary bank: **Income**, **Owner Pay**, and **Business Expenses**. At your second bank, you've set up your out of sight, out of mind savings accounts: **Profit** and **Tax**. If you haven't set up the bank accounts yet, I'll hold my breath until you do. Do it now! Don't wait too long, I have four children counting on me to keep breathing. Go set those accounts up now, before I turn blue.

Ahhh. It feels good to breathe again. Now it's time to nickname each account online. With these nicknames in place, you'll know exactly where your money should go. Presto. You've set up a system to indicate how much money is available to spend in each area of your business.

Once you've set up your accounts at the bank, the bank summary section of your online banking login page should look like the list below. Of course, the last four digits of your account numbers will be different than my example numbers. When you get a commission check, all the money you receive goes into the **Income** account first.

> **Income** *5615
> **Profit** *4313
> **Owner Pay** *2617
> **Tax** *3861
> **Business Expenses** *7632

TAKE ACTION: SET UP YOUR BANK ACCOUNTS

Set up your bank accounts before you read any further. Without the five bank accounts, you will not be able to use the system. None of the knowledge in the following pages will do you any good until you use the system, so set up those bank accounts now.

CHAPTER 5:

LEARN HOW YOUR BUSINESS SPENDS ITS MONEY

When you list a house, one of the most important steps you perform is a walk-through of the property. You look for everything special about the home. You also develop a punch list of improvements needed to make the home move-in ready. Every house has some of both. In this chapter, you'll perform a walk-through of your Dream Home Business and assess its move-in readiness.

Your Dream Home Business is composed of two main sections—the roof and the house. The house is where most of the value should reside. The roof is designed to protect the house so that you can enjoy it. In your real estate business, the greater the amount of money that flows to your house, the better off you'll be.

The roof represents all the business expenses you incur, whether they be contract labor, vendors, lead generation, or employees. Basically, any money spent to run your business belongs to the roof.

The house includes the following:

- Foundation: Owner Pay
- First floor: Profit
- Second floor: Tax

In this chapter, I'll guide you through the process of determining how much you currently spend in each component of your Dream Home Business. We'll start with the house first and then move on to the roof. Once we've completed the walk-through, you'll understand what works and where to make improvements.

In Chapter 3, you calculated your Personal Lifestyle Number. You will use a similar process to determine where the money flows in each area of your Dream Home Business. First, you will calculate your owner pay, profit, and tax. Then you will calculate your business expenses. The final step of the walk-through is the Instant Assessment, which will summarize how much you make and where all the money flows. Once you know how much flows to you and how much the business uses, you'll be empowered to make adjustments that will allow you to pay yourself fairly, pay your taxes on time, and reduce underperforming business expenses.

OWNER PAY

As owner pay is the foundation, it's important to determine how much you pay yourself. Look at the last three months of your business bank statements to find any amount you paid yourself with a paycheck and/or an owner distribution or draw. Other items to include in owner pay are:

- Luxury vehicles
- Owner health insurance
- Company retirement contributions to the owner
- Personal business trips
- Any expense run through the business for a tax write-off

TABLE 6: OWNER PAY					
	Month 1	Month 2	Month 3	Total	Average
Owner Pay					

TABLE 7: OWNER PAY EXAMPLE					
	Month 1	Month 2	Month 3	Total	Average
Owner Pay	4,000	5,000	6,000	15,000	5,000

Do not include any federal or state income tax payments you made via quarterly estimates or from your paycheck. They are not owner pay. They are tax payments and will be included in the Tax table (Table 10).

Steps to calculate owner pay:

1. Highlight all the owner pay items for Month 1.
2. Add them together to get your total owner pay for the month.
3. Enter the total owner pay into the Month 1 box of Table 6 above.
4. Repeat steps 2 and 3 for the other two months.
5. Add together the amounts for the three months and enter the total amount in the Total box.
6. Divide the total by three and enter the amount in the Average box.
7. Compare the average with the Personal Lifestyle Number you calculated in Table 5, Chapter 3.
8. Determine if your current owner pay is sufficient to cover your Personal Lifestyle Number.

PROFIT

Profit is the reward of a successful business. Profit only occurs when it is paid to you, the owner. If you leave it in the business or reinvest it, you don't have a profit yet. When you take profit out of your business, you prevent Clyde, The Human Problem, from convincing you to spend everything you make on business expenses. Taking your profits is a key activity that will increase the value of your Dream Home Business.

Unless you have an established process to distribute profits to yourself regularly, you will not record profits in Table 8 (this is why Table 9 has a zero in every space). Any money you paid to yourself before should be included in owner pay. No need to fret; taking profits is a new concept for most business owners before they learn about Profit First. I ran my business for eight years without taking any profits.

Steps to calculate Profit:

1. Highlight all the profit payments for Month 1.
2. Add them together to get your total profit for the month.
3. Enter the total profit into the Month 1 box.
4. Repeat steps two and three for the other two months.
5. Add together the amounts for the three months and enter the total in the Total box.

TABLE 8: PROFIT					
	Month 1	Month 2	Month 3	Total	Average
Profit					

TABLE 9: PROFIT EXAMPLE					
	Month 1	Month 2	Month 3	Total	Average
Profit	0	0	0	0	0

6. Divide the total by three and enter the amount in the Average box.

TAX

The tax bill is an expense that is despised by many real estate agents. It tends to be the last thing anyone wants to think about, let alone pay. Often, it is higher than expected. Other times, it comes as a surprise to agents because they paid their estimated taxes each quarter. Most tax preparers create quarterly tax estimates based on last year's tax bill. If your income doubles this year, wouldn't it make sense for your tax bill to double as well? Unless you and your accountant update your quarterly estimates throughout the year, you may be in for a tax surprise next April.

If you receive a paycheck, you will need copies of your pay stubs from the last three months, in addition to the last three months of bank statements, in order to calculate your tax.

Steps to calculate tax:
1. Highlight all the federal and state estimated income tax payments for Month 1.
2. Highlight all the federal and state income tax from your pay stubs from Month 1.

TABLE 10: TAX					
	Month 1	Month 2	Month 3	Total	Average
Tax					

TABLE 11: TAX EXAMPLE					
	Month 1	Month 2	Month 3	Total	Average
Tax	2,200	7,000	2,200	11,400	3,800

3. Add the tax estimates from step 1 and tax from your paychecks from step 2 together to get the total tax for the month.
4. Enter the total tax into the Month 1 box.
5. Repeat steps 1 through 4 for the other two months.
6. Add together the amounts for the three months and enter the total in the Total box.
7. Divide the amount in the Total box by three and enter it in the Average box.

BUSINESS EXPENSES

You're now at the roof of your Dream Home Business. There are only four types of spending in your business. You've calculated three of them, which means that everything else is a business expense. The easiest way to calculate your business expenses is to take total spending for the month and subtract owner pay, profit, and tax from that total.

Here are the steps to calculate your business expenses:

1. Add the data from Table 6 to the Owner Pay row of Table 12.
2. Add the data from Table 8 to the Profit row of Table 12.
3. Add the data from Table 10 to the Tax row of Table 12.
4. Look at the summary section on the bank statement for Month 1. Potentially, you will see three types of spending: checks, bank fees, and withdrawals. Some banks show the total amount for all three, which makes your job easier. If they appear as more than one line item in the summary section, add them together to get the total spending.

TABLE 12: BUSINESS EXPENSES					
	Month 1	Month 2	Month 3	Total	Average
Total Spending					
Owner Pay					
Profit					
Tax					
Business Expenses					

5. Enter the total spending into the Month 1 column of Table 12.
6. Repeat steps 4 and 5 for the other two months.
7. Add together the amounts for the three months and enter the total in the Total column.
8. Divide the total by three and enter the amount in the Average column.
9. For Month 1, subtract owner pay, profit, and tax from total spending.
10. Enter the amount in the Business Expenses box under Month 1.
11. Repeat steps 9 and 10 for the other two months.
12. Add together the amounts for the three months and enter the total in the Total column.
13. Divide the total by three and enter the amount in the Average column.

Once you complete Table 12, you know how much you spend, on average, in each area of your business. In the future, you may not need to complete Tables 6, 8, and 10. I took you through those three tables so you could isolate the expenses

	Month 1	Month 2	Month 3	Total	Average
TABLE 13: BUSINESS EXPENSES EXAMPLE					
Total Spending	12,000	18,000	14,000	44,000	14,667
Owner Pay	4,000	5,000	6,000	15,000	5,000
Profit	0	0	0	0	0
Tax	2,200	7,000	2,200	11,400	3,800
Business Expenses	5,800	6,000	5,800	17,600	5,867

without having to hire a bookkeeper or enter everything into accounting software.

The goal with this exercise is to get a ballpark estimate. You do not need an exact number. Close enough is close enough. I would rather have you calculate a ballpark estimate in ten minutes than take thirty days to get exact numbers. If you've never kept accurate accounting records, it will take a while to get exact numbers; and in order for you to be successful with Profit First for Real Estate Agents, I need you to take the right financial steps today. Don't wait until your bookkeeper or accountant gets your books cleaned up. While accurate accounting records are important, they are not necessary at this stage of setting up the system.

You now know how to calculate your monthly owner pay, profit, tax, and business expenses. All the work you did was to complete the Average column. These numbers are based on real data. You no longer need to guess how much you spend in each area.

INCOME

We've spent the entire chapter so far focusing on all the money that left your business. It's been a lot of work. You deserve a high five. Raise your hand high and wave those fingers so you and I can slap our hands together. We'll shift gears and calculate your average income. Then you'll have all you need to finish the walk-through of your Dream Home Business. You'll repeat the process you used to calculate each of your spending types earlier in this chapter. Now you focus on the fun part—all the commissions you brought in. You'll input this information in Table 14.

1. Look at the total deposits on your bank statement for Month 1.
2. Enter the total deposits into the Month 1 box.
3. Repeat steps 1 and 2 for the other two months.
4. Add together the amounts for the three months and enter the total in the Total column.
5. Divide the total by three and enter the amount in the Average column.

TABLE 14: INCOME

	Month 1	Month 2	Month 3	Total	Average
Income					

TABLE 15: INCOME EXAMPLE

	Month 1	Month 2	Month 3	Total	Average
Income	20,000	17,000	23,000	60,000	20,000

INSTANT ASSESSMENT

You already have the ingredients to complete the Instant Assessment. The Instant Assessment is a financial checkup for your business, similar to when your physician checks your vital signs. They measure your weight, blood pressure, and temperature and check your reflexes. The vital signs reveal critical information about your body's health. Likewise, the Instant Assessment gives you the critical information you need to gauge your business's health. Either your business is healthy or unhealthy. Once you know the health status of your business, it's time to look for items that negatively affect your health and eliminate them.

Once you remove the unhealthy aspects of your business, you give it room to grow. Imagine walking down the sidewalk, tripping on a crack, falling, and breaking your arm. You feel pain. Your arm is unhealthy. You can bemoan the crack in the sidewalk; you can hire a lawyer to sue the sidewalk maker. However, neither of these activities will heal your broken arm.

To heal it, you need a physician to reset the arm so both sides of the fracture site line up, then put your arm in a cast to immobilize it until it is healed. The first step toward healing a broken arm is to fix what is broken. Until it is fixed, you will not regain full use of your arm.

Unhealthy business finances will not become healthy unless you remove the cause of their poor health. When unhealthy money habits weigh down the business, money leaks out. The Instant Assessment informs you of how healthy or unhealthy your business is. To complete the Instant Assessment, you will refer to the amounts in the Average columns of Tables 6, 8, 10, and 12 (the last three months).

Steps to complete the Instant Assessment:

1. Enter the average income from Table 14 in the Income box in Table 16.

TABLE 16: INSTANT ASSESSMENT		
	Amount	Current Percentage
Income		
Profit		
Owner Pay		
Tax		
Business Expenses		

2. Enter the average owner pay from Table 6 in the Owner Pay box in Table 16.
3. Enter the average profit from Table 8 in the Profit box in Table 16.
4. Enter the tax from Table 10 in the Tax box in Table 16.
5. Enter business expenses from Table 12 in the Business Expenses box in Table 16.
6. Compute the owner pay percentage by dividing the owner pay amount by the income amount.
7. Repeat step 6 for profit, tax, and business expenses.

TABLE 17: INSTANT ASSESSMENT EXAMPLE		
	Amount	Current Percentage
Income	20,000	
Profit	0	0%
Owner Pay	5,000	25%
Tax	3,800	19%
Business Expenses	5,867	29%

	A	B	C	D	E	F
			TABLE 18: TARGET ALLOCATION PERCENTAGES (TAPS)			
Net Commission Income Range	$0 – 250K	$250K – $500K	$500K – $1M	$1M – $5M	$5M – $10M	$10M – $50
Net Commission Income	100%	100%	100%	100%	100%	100%
Profit	5%	10%	15%	20%	18%	17%
Owner Pay	50%	35%	20%	10%	7%	3%
Tax	15%	15%	15%	15%	15%	15%
Business Expenses	30%	40%	50%	55%	60%	65%

HOW TARGET ALLOCATION PERCENTAGES WORK

Target allocation percentages (TAPs) are the targets you'll use to improve your profitability. With the Instant Assessment, you determined what percentage of income is spent in each area of your Dream Home Business.

Table 18 shows the six tiers for the TAPs.

1. When a company earns less than $250,000 in revenue per year, it typically has one employee: you. You are the key and usually the only employee (with some contractors, part-timers, or possibly one other full-timer). Many are at this stage, and if they elect to stay that way (with no other employees), they should be able to increase the profit and pay percentages beyond what I have listed because they don't have the expense of employees or the need to incur the expenses required to support multiple employees.

2. At \$250,000 to \$500,000, you may have employees, in which case basic systems will be necessary, like a shared customer relationship management system for your team, equipment, etc.; plus, you need to pay your people, so your business expenses increase. Owner pay adjusts down (and will continue to do so) as you take your first step toward being a little less of an employee and a little more of a shareholder. This is when other people start to do the work, and you get the benefit of the profits via your distributions.

3. At \$500,000 to \$1,000,000, the growth trend and patterns continue with more systems and more people. Focus on increasing profits because, for so many businesses, the growth from \$1,000,000 to \$5,000,000 is the hardest. You want some cash reserves.

4. From \$1,000,000 to \$5,000,000, systems are no longer added because they are nice to have; they become mandatory. You can't keep it all in your head anymore. Often, the biggest investment in the business needs to happen at this time, as all your knowledge needs to be converted to systems, processes, and checklists. This means that larger allocations must be put toward business expenses. This is when you no longer do most of the work; this is when, if your business is to grow, a significant portion of your time is spent working on the business—not in it—and the rest of your time is spent selling the big projects.

5. At \$5,000,000 to \$10,000,000, a management team typically enters a company to bring it to the next stage, and a clear second tier of management starts to form. The owner focuses more and more on their special strengths. The owner is on a consistent payroll, and the

majority of their take-home income comes from the profitability of the company, not the salary they take.

6. At $10,000,000 to $50,000,000, a business will often stabilize and achieve predictable growth. The owner's income comes almost entirely from profit distributions. Owners' salaries are relative to their roles, but are typically insignificant. Businesses of this size can leverage efficiency in big ways to maximize profitability.

DETERMINE YOUR TARGET ALLOCATION PERCENTAGES

You now have your current allocation percentages. I recommend that you start slowly with your target allocation percentages. You are establishing a new system, and it is better to start slowly and experience success than blast off, fail miserably, and quit before you have the chance to succeed.

Let's take a moment to address income so you and I are referencing the same language. If you don't have a team, you will probably not have to split commissions with anyone unless you pay a fee to someone who sent you a referral. If you have a team, you and your team members will be splitting commissions. When you look at total team production, you will be looking at gross commission income. However, not all of this belongs to you. The cost of sales will be the amount of commission you split with your agents on your team and referrals sent to agents outside of your team. When you subtract cost of sales from gross commission income, you arrive at net commission income.

You will want to focus on your net commission income. This is the real revenue your business earns. How you spend your net commission income will determine how healthy your real estate business is.

When I create a Profit First Rollout Plan for one of my clients, the first thing I ask them is if enough money is allocated to owner pay. What if your current owner pay allocation is $3,000 and you need $5,000 to support your lifestyle? You should consider a few scenarios—either increasing revenue, decreasing expenses, or both.

First, do you need $5,000 a month? Look at your personal expenses. Are there any expenses you can reduce for the next couple months until your business earns more? If you need $5,000 a month, your first goal is to increase revenue and reduce expenses so you can pay yourself $5,000 a month. I've stated multiple times throughout this book that while I talk about profit first, we need to pay the owner first, before the business receives a profit.

Which expenses will you reduce so your owner pay amount equals your Personal Lifestyle Number? How can you increase revenue now to ensure that you have enough owner pay?

The next step is to determine your profit percentage. Most of the time I start with 1% for the first three months. This establishes the right behavior to ensure that your business is permanently profitable. This percentage may appear too low, but don't despair. We need you to move in the right direction first. As you get used to the Profit First for Real Estate Agents system, we can increase the percentage as you gain momentum. I would rather have you start with small steps and build cash in your **Profit** bank account. This is better than taking Goliath-sized steps. You're in this for the long game. Start slowly. You will learn what works and what doesn't work while the stakes are still low.

The next step is to allocate money to the **Tax** account. Your tax bill is always just around the corner. You need to set money aside so you don't have to worry about an IRS agent knocking on your door, flashing their badge, and asking why you didn't pay your bill on time. Many of the real estate agents I've talked with state that a surprise tax bill is one of their biggest stressors. But, just like clockwork, your tax bill will come due—and you must pay your taxes. To calculate an initial tax percentage, review your most recent tax returns. What was the total tax due for last year?

If you paid $8,000 to taxes last year, assume that your net commission income for this year will be the same amount as last year. With your net commission income at $100,000, you paid $8,000 in taxes. Your tax percentage based on net commission income is 8% ($8,000 ÷ $100,000), so your initial target allocation percentage for tax should be 8%. I recommend you consult your tax advisor to determine where to set your tax percentage.

Let's say your personal living expenses are $8,000 a month. With the owner pay TAP at 50% of net commission income, your business needs to generate monthly net commission income equal to $16,000. However, if you reduce your personal living expenses to $5,000 a month, your business only needs to generate net commission income equal to $10,000. As your business income grows, more money is available for you. As a result, you can return to your previous personal spending level.

Use the Target Allocation Percentages table (Table 18) to complete the Column 5 TAPs in Table 19.

Complete Column 4, current allocation percentages (CAPs) for Q1. You will use these percentages for the next three months.

A couple of common questions I hear from many real estate agents I work with are, "Am I spending the right amount of

TABLE 19: CURRENT ALLOCATION PERCENTAGES (CAPS)				
	Actual Amount	Actual %	CAPs Q1	TAPs
Gross Commission Income				
Cost of Sales				
Net Commission Income	$100,000			
Profit	$0			5%
Owner Pay	$30,000	30%		50%
Tax	$5,000	5%		15%
Business Expenses	$65,000	65%		30%

money? What are other real estate agents doing?" The CAPs table above should give you clear idea of how much money you can afford to spend in each of the four main areas of your business. Remember, you get a new money pie with each commission check. It's your job to slice it so that each of the four areas of business—profit, owner pay, tax, and business expenses—are fed enough but not too much.

SMALL STEPS LEAD TO BIG OUTCOMES

There is an old Chinese proverb that says, "You have to eat an elephant bite by bite." It would be impossible for any human to eat a whole elephant in one sitting. Just imagine how bloated you would feel after an elephant-eating extravaganza.

Most people walk the equivalent of two marathon distances every month. The length of one marathon is 26.2 miles; two marathons equal 52.4 miles. The average American walks one-and-a-half to two miles per day. Multiply that daily mileage times thirty days and you get 52.4 to sixty miles per month. I bet you didn't realize that you complete two marathons every month before you read this book.

One of the big misconceptions held by many who haven't *run* a marathon is that everyone runs the whole time. That isn't the case. Or at least it wasn't with me. I switched between running and walking for each of the seven marathons I completed. In fact, during my first marathon, some of the competitors went the entire distance without putting a single foot on the ground because they were in wheelchairs. When it comes to completing a marathon, the most important aspect is persisting until you arrive at the finish line. The first person and the last person to cross the finish line have two things in common: They both completed the race and they both get the finisher's medal.

If you want to run a complete marathon in one day, you need to train for at least four months prior to race day. It would be foolhardy to join a marathon without any training. In the best-case scenario, your body would ache. In the worst-case scenario, you would take a permanent dirt nap. You don't have to be a hardcore runner to complete a marathon if you break the distance into bite-size pieces that fit it into your daily life. Don't attempt to do too much at once.

When I decided to run my first marathon, I did not run 26.2 miles the very next day. My first step was to run two miles. Then I ran another two miles a few days later. Then I ran another two miles a few days later. For two months, I ran two miles three times a week to give my body time to build up strength and stamina.

It's the same with your Profit First Rollout Plan. When you make a permanent change to guarantee profitability, will it be detrimental to your success if it takes a few more months to achieve your goal? No. One step forward is still one step forward. The direction you are headed is more important than your speed. Give your business a chance to adjust to the new financial regimen. If you cut your expenses by 50% tomorrow, you may cut spending that is vital to your business. It will be too quick. It will lead to failure. I don't want you to fail. Hold some grace for yourself. Give your business space and time to adjust to your new money management system.

I would rather have you take twenty-four months to get to target profitability than bust a gut as you scramble to get there in one month, flame out, fail, and get discouraged because you tried to do too much in too little time. It will take a minute to transform your business from unprofitable to profitable.

If you trust the system and work it, you will achieve success. One of the biggest lessons I learned when I ran my first marathon is that the key to completing a marathon is to put one foot in front of the other, and to continue doing that for 26.2 miles. There were times during the race when I stopped running because my legs were too tired, and I wanted to quit. But I was focused on the goal of finishing the race, so instead of quitting, I walked. I got bored with the journey. I shed a few tears. However, I continued to put one foot in front of the other until I reached the finish line.

My favorite story from childhood is "The Hare & the Tortoise," one of Aesop's fables. Here is the version presented by the Library of Congress:

A Hare was making fun of the Tortoise one day for being so slow.

"Do you ever get anywhere?" he asked with a mocking laugh.

"Yes," replied the Tortoise, "and I get there sooner than you think. I'll run you a race and prove it."

The Hare was much amused at the idea of running a race with the Tortoise, but for the fun of the thing he agreed. So the Fox, who had consented to act as judge, marked the distance and started the runners off.

The Hare was soon far out of sight, and to make the Tortoise feel very deeply how ridiculous it was for him to try a race with a Hare, he lay down beside the course to take a nap until the Tortoise should catch up.

The Tortoise meanwhile kept going slowly but steadily, and, after a time, passed the place where the Hare was sleeping. But the Hare slept on very peacefully; and when at last he did wake up, the Tortoise was near the goal. The Hare now ran his swiftest, but he could not overtake the Tortoise in time.

The race is not always to the swift.[15]

---

[15] Aesop, "The Hare & the Tortoise." Reprinted from the Library of Congress website and adapted from Milo Winter's *The Aesop for Children: with Pictures* (Chicago, IL: Rand McNally, 1919). http://read.gov/aesop/025.html,

CHAPTER 6:

THE PROFIT FIRST
ROLLOUT PLAN

The previous five chapters gave you the foundational knowledge you needed to simplify and understand your business finances. With this foundation in place, we will now build out the best money system for your business. I'll take you through some simple steps so you can accomplish the following:

- Gain clarity on how your business spends
- Develop targets to get you to ideal profitability
- Build your initial Profit First Rollout Plan
- Envision a better business

You will reallocate your net commission income so you spend the proper amount for owner pay, profit, tax, and business expenses. Establish the current allocation percentages (CAPs) in your business today, and you will achieve results with your very next commission check.

In this chapter, you'll learn how the Profit First system works. Don't fret if it feels uncomfortable at first. It might take a bit of work and time to get used to the system. Remember when you were learning scripts to use when calling people? You probably stumbled over your words a few times. But you stuck with it until it became natural for you. You learned the sales communications skills you needed. In this chapter, you'll learn the skills you need to keep more money in your pocket.

You remember Bonnie and Clyde, The Devious Duo. Bonnie's job is to distract you so Clyde can pick your pocket. I'm reminded of the story of the Three Little Pigs. The first pig built his house out of straw. The wolf blew down the straw house with little effort. The pig ran away and joined his brother, who had built his house out of bricks. No matter how hard the wolf blew at the brick house, he could not prevail.

You may have struggled with money because you were working with a straw house. With Profit First, you will build a brick house for your Dream Home Business—one that will prevent Bonnie and Clyde from gaining access to the money you work so hard to earn.

CAPS — START OUT EASY

You've got your bank accounts set up, and you've renamed them to give you clarity on how much money you have to spend. When you completed your Instant Assessment, you determined your target allocation percentages (TAPs) for each account. The TAPs are where you want to take your business. However, you're not there yet. There are improvements to make before your business will arrive at the TAPs. We'll start off with manageable tweaks that give you breathing room to adjust to the new system and assign a new percentage to each account. These percentages are called CAPs (current allocation percentages). It will take some work and time to transition from your CAPs to the TAPs.

For your initial CAPs, you will start with Day Zero percentages. These are the ones you've used prior to

TABLE 20: DAY ONE CAPS			
	Day Zero	Adjustment	Day One
Profit	0%	+1%	1%
Owner Pay	30%	+1%	31%
Tax	5%	+1%	6%
Business Expenses	65%	-3%	62%

implementing Profit First, the ones you plugged into your Instant Assessment as spending percentages for profit, owner pay, tax, and business expenses. Add 1% to Day Zero percentages to get your Day One percentages. This may mean you have a goose egg on Day Zero for some of your accounts. For example, if your profit sometimes shows up and other times is nonexistent, your profit (until today) has been zero. Your initial Day One profit will be 1% CAP (0% on Day Zero + 1% starting today). You'll nudge it up once each quarter as your grow your profits. Use the Day One CAPs for the remainder of this quarter, whether it ends in one week or twelve.

If you paid yourself 30% of revenue, your Day Zero owner pay percentage will be 30% and you will add 1% to get 31% for Day One owner pay CAP.

If in the past, tax payments from your business were 5% of revenues, your Day Zero tax percentage will be 5%. You will add 1% to Day Zero to arrive at 6% for your Day One tax CAP. Your TAPs will probably be higher than Day One CAPs, but you need to start where you are now and move in the right direction toward your target profitability.

Now you will reduce your business expenses percentage by the total percentage changes you made to the other three accounts. In our example, profit, owner pay, and tax each went up by 1%, for a total of 3%. Consequently, you will reduce your business expenses by 3%.

You are easing into your new system. The first step to implementing Profit First is to get started with something easy. The easier you make this for yourself in the beginning, the better your chances of success will be.

When I first learned how to ride a bike, I fell over constantly and scraped my elbows and knees. It was painful and I wanted to quit. My mother installed training wheels on the rear axle so I could have support as I learned how to balance myself on two wheels. Guess what—I stopped getting scabs on my elbows. After a few weeks, I shed the training wheels and learned how to pop a wheelie. I learned how to ride a bike more than forty years ago (gosh this makes me feel ancient), and now I zoom down the street with ease.

Your first quarter of Profit First is your training period, during which you will adjust to the automatic money management system. After you master the small steps, you'll build momentum, and with each new quarter, you'll move yourself closer to your TAPs.

Before you started Profit First, all your money was in one pot and you had no clarity on where the money went. Now you'll need to learn how to gain control of your money with small changes. You have several more bank accounts now, and that will be an adjustment for you. You may stumble; it's normal to stumble with something new. And it's better to stumble with small adjustments now than with big adjustments later. Once you master the small changes, you'll be off to the races. Twelve months from now, you'll be surprised at the progress you've achieved.

Most businesses have never paid the owners a profit. At best, they give the owners a salary. In other instances, owners pull money out whenever there is some extra in the bank. They have no idea if the money they take out is owner pay or profit. You may have had a P&L statement which declared you had a profit, but were left perplexed about where that phantom profit disappeared to. Unless you specifically gave yourself a profit check, you did not get a profit.

Profit only exists when it is paid to you, the business owner. Few real estate agencies have a history of distributing profits to the owners. Don't get upset or discouraged about not having a profit. You are not alone. Everyone struggles with profit in the beginning; there is no reason for you, me, or anyone else to shame or judge you about it. Start with where you are and leave yesterday in the past, where it belongs. We are in this together, to improve your life and bring your business to prosperity. Again, unless you gave yourself a designated profit check in the last three months, your Day Zero profit percentage will be 0%.

Your business expenses Day Zero percentage will be everything else. If you have a P&L statement, look at your total expenses. To calculate your business expenses Day Zero percentage, divide the total expenses by your income.

Don't worry about having these numbers correct down to the last penny. You simply need a starting point, a place to begin. It is more important to start now than it is to have perfect numbers. Once you've started, you will be able to make adjustment along the way. If you don't get started, you won't be able to make adjustments. And you can't make adjustments without taking action, so get moving now.

In the last chapter, we created nicknames for each of our bank accounts. Now that you have your Day Zero CAPs, we'll be adding those to the online nicknames of each bank account. For example, before adding the CAPs to the nickname, your **Profit** account looks like this:

Profit *4313

When you add a Day Zero profit CAP of 0%, the nickname will look like this:

Profit 0% *4313

Add the CAPs to all of your bank account nicknames.

For many businesses, Day Zero percentages might look something like this:

Income *5615
Profit 0% *4313
Owner Pay 15% *2617
Tax 0% *3861
Business Expenses 121% *7632

Easing into the first quarter of Profit First, this example business could add 1% to Day Zero profit, 1% to owner pay, and 1% to tax, and reduce business expenses by 3%.

Day One CAPs would then look like this:

Income *5615
Profit 1% *4313
Owner Pay 16% *2617
Tax 1% *3861
Business Expenses 118% *7632

As you review these percentages, you will see that, historically, this business hasn't had a profit. The owner received 15% of income and business expenses were 121% of income. Does anything about that strike you as odd? When we add owner pay and business expenses, we get 136%. The business spent 136% of the income it received. In other words, it spent 36% more than it earned that year. Where did the money come from to cover the extra spending? It came from credit cards and loans the owner made to the business.

An excellent way to run a business into the ground is to overspend, then borrow more money and overspend some more. At some point the business will be broken beyond repair. Someone will need to put that business out of its misery.

Who in the world would be so stupid as to operate a business with such poor money management? I'll tell you who. A man named Damon Yudichak.

These were the CAPs I had in December, 2009, after my first full year in business as a CPA. My business bled money, and I didn't pay myself enough to support my family. To keep my business "afloat," I pumped my personal savings into a cash-eating monster. I deluded myself with thoughts of all the money I would make during the spring months of tax season. While my income during the first half of 2010 surpassed my total income for the prior year, my business expenses were too high. I allowed my business to be caught in a cycle of spending more as it made more.

Years later, the words of my business coach, Wayne Salmans—"You can't out-earn stupid"—rang at my core as I remembered how stupid I had been in my first two years of business. When I paid myself, it was only if I had enough left over after I paid everyone else. I'd neglected the fundamental truth that I was the most important person in my business and, as such, I deserved to be paid first and best.

I had to take drastic action. It was time to stop the bleeding immediately. After pounding my head against the wall for the five hundredth time (I'm being kind to myself—it was probably more like the four thousandth time) I ultimately learned the following lesson.

Total spending—including profit, owner pay, tax, and business expenses—cannot exceed income.

If it does, you will never get ahead. A business will not prosper if it spends more than it makes. I came to this realization in July, 2010, when my credit cards were maxed out and my personal savings were depleted. I backed myself against the wall because I couldn't get money from myself anymore. The only way to get money was to run my business profitably. I made two fundamental changes:

1. I paid myself first with every dollar that came into my business. I set up my **Owner Pay** bank account and nicknamed it the Damon bank account. As soon as I made a deposit, I moved 10% from my **Business Expenses** account to my Damon account.
2. I forced my business to function within the remaining amount in the **Business Expenses** account. When I had a buying decision to make, I looked at my **Business Expenses** account to see if I had enough money to make the purchase. If I didn't have enough money, I had to do without, get creative, and come up with a new alternative.

After the first six months of 2010, my CAPs were:

Income *5615
Profit 0% (TAP 5%) *4313
Owner Pay 38% (TAP 50%) *2617
Tax 0% (TAP 15%) *3861
Business Expenses 66% (TAP 30%) *7632

My total percentages were still more than 100% (Owner Pay 38% + Business Expenses 66% = 104%). I had slowed the bleeding, but not stopped it yet. I still had some work to do to break even. I adjusted my percentages by adding 1% to profit and 1% to tax, and reducing business expenses and owner pay by 3% each. Overall, my total spending stayed at 104% of total income. However, my business expenses were lower, and I was paying myself more. It was an important step in the right direction. The accounts then looked like this:

Income *5615
Profit 1% (TAP 5%) *4313
Owner Pay 39% (TAP 50%) *2617
Tax 1% (TAP 15%) *3861
Business Expenses 63% (TAP 30%) *7632

I've shared my personal example with you to give you some hope. Everyone struggles with money at some point in their lives. That's part of how we learn about it. One of the great lessons my mother taught me was, "Tomorrow will be a better day." If it feels like Bonnie is using a jackhammer on your head to inflict the most pain possible, remember—it won't last forever.

Tomorrow will be a better day.

Now that you've seen how yours truly obliterated his finances and lived another day to write a book about it, I'll give you an example of how you could adjust your CAPS from Day Zero to Day One.

Hopefully you are in a better position than the one I found myself in during my first few years of business. You'll have the liberty to ease into the Profit First system. You'll be able to learn from my mistakes. Correct your business before it's too miserable to continue.

Now you are moving your business in the right direction. You increased the money you will receive for profit and owner pay, and set aside money for the tax bill, by reducing your business expenses. Your business is already using its money more wisely. You will get ahead financially. Isn't this what a business should do for you?

MAKE YOUR FIRST BANK TRANSFER

Robert Plant, the great singer, said, "The past is a stepping-stone, not a millstone."[16] You would not have realized how important profits are without your prior experience. Consider everything you've done before today as a stepping-stone to a new and better business, a business in which you are intentional about your profitability—not just in thought; you now have a systematic approach to transform those thoughts into reality. Starting today, you will guarantee that your business is profitable because you will capture your profit before anyone has a chance to steal it from you.

Today is the best day to take your profits first. You must act now to put your money system in motion. Don't skim through these words without doing the work. Your knowledge of how Profit First works will not improve your business. Your actions will improve your business.

Look at the balance of your primary business bank account. You should have renamed this the **Business Expenses** account. Calculate the total of any outstanding checks or payments you have made from this account. Subtract this amount from the balance in the **Business Expenses** account. Transfer the remaining amount to your **Income** account. For example, if

---

[16] "Robert Plant Quotes," BrainyQuote.com, BrainyMedia Inc, accessed October 17, 2021, https://www.brainyquote.com/quotes/robert_plant_472881.

you had $5,000 and your outstanding payments are $2,100, you would transfer $2,900 to your **Income** account, leaving $2,100 to cover the outstanding payments.

Now you will do your first bank transfer. Divide the money in the **Income** account into the other accounts (**Profit, Owner Pay, Tax**, and **Business Expenses**) based on your Day One CAPs. This is the inaugural bank transfer. From this day forward, the only time money will move out of your **Income** account will be in the form of bank transfers to the other accounts.

When we continue with our example, your transfers would look like this:

> **Income** *5615 → It had $2,900 and goes to $0 because all money is transferred to the **Profit, Owner Pay, Tax**, and **Business Expenses** accounts based on your percentages.
> **Profit** 1% (TAP 5%) *4313 → $29 goes here.
> **Owner Pay** 35% (TAP 50%) *2617 → $1,015 goes here.
> **Tax** 1% (TAP 15%) *3861 → $29 goes here.
> **Business Expenses** 63% (TAP 30%) *7632 → $1,827 goes here.

Now you know how much money is used in each area of your business. I was disturbed, back in 2010, when I saw that more than half of my income went to pay business expenses. At least I finally knew where I stood, though. Before I used my Profit First system, I was a blind man in the business wilderness. Money leaked out of my business just as quickly as it came in. Now I have a system that diverts fund toward me, so I keep a portion of all I earn. Now, with the best money system in place, I know where my money is spent. Additionally, I know that the way to increase my share of the money pie is to reduce the business expenses slice.

Start your day with the question: What can I do to increase my profits today?

You have an incredibly powerful idea generator called a brain. When you ask it the right questions, you will get ideas to improve your business. Here are some other questions to ponder:

- What can I do to reduce expenses?
- How can I make more profitable sales?
- What new strategic partnerships can I generate?
- What can I do to reduce waste?

You've now made your first bank transfer. If you have some money to deposit, put it in the bank and do another bank transfer. Repetition is the path to mastery.

YOUR FIRST CELEBRATION

Kapow!! You did it. Pat yourself on the back. You are now a Profit First Real Estate Agent! Very few real estate agents set anything aside for their profits, but you are not leaving your money to chance. Almost everyone complains about making a lot and not having anything to show for it. You, however, have begun to pay yourself first, harvest your profits, and ensure that your taxes are taken care of. You're in the driver's seat of your business now. As Plato said, "The beginning is the most important part of the work."[17] You've now finished the first step toward building a super profitable real estate business. Find a way to celebrate your win today.

---

[17] Plato, *The Republic*, trans. Benjamin Jowett (New York, NY: Books, Inc., 1943).

CUT EXPENSES

One of the quickest ways to improve profitability is to reduce unproductive expenses. We all spend money that provides minimal value to our businesses. For example, I remember a conversation I had with my banker over lunch when I talked with her about Profit First.

"Damon," she said, "I have three gym memberships and it's been more than a month since I went to the gym. I don't need three gym memberships. I'll start with canceling two of them."

Many businesses can easily cut 10 to 20% of business expenses without damaging the business. While it may be daunting to cut expenses, I want you to recognize the alternative result. Imagine yourself next to campfire. See yourself opening your wallet and dumping money into the flames. Smell the aroma of burning cash. Watch as the flames consume it, turning it into ash and smoke. Which is more painful, cutting expenses or watching your money go up in flames?

When you created your Day One CAPs, your goal was to reduce business expenses by at least 3% so you could allocate 1% to your **Profit**, **Owner Pay**, and **Tax** accounts. Let's turn that 3% reduction into reality. Let's say your Day Zero business expenses percentage was 66%, and we want to lower it to 63%. Assume your average monthly commissions total $8,000. Prior to today, 66%, or $5,280, of your commissions went to business expenses. How would your business be different if you only spend 63% of your commissions on business expenses? That equals $5,040. To achieve your business expenses percentage reduction, you need to reduce monthly business expenses by $240 before the end of the quarter.

Let's make this as easy as possible. Assume you just started the quarter and have twelve weeks before the next quarter begins. To reach your goal, you need to reduce business expenses by twenty dollars a week. What can you do to reduce business expenses by twenty dollars this week? How about next week? How about the following week? Break the big amount into smaller amounts and it becomes much easier.

BANK TRANSFER FREQUENCY

As real estate agents grow their businesses, the frequency of when they receive commissions varies. If you have less than twenty transactions per year, you may only have one or two deposits per month. If you fall into this camp, I recommend you do your bank transfer each time you receive a commission check. This way, you allocate the money to the proper accounts. You'll know how much money you have available for business expenses based on how much is in the **Business Expenses** account.

Once your business grows to the point where you regularly deposit commissions more than three times a month, it's time to establish the twice monthly bank transfer schedule. You'll continue to deposit your commissions to your **Income** account as you've done so far, but instead of doing a bank transfer on the same day, you will wait until the tenth of the month and the twenty-fifth of the month.

Here is how the process works:

Step 1: Deposit all commissions to your **Income** account.

Step 2: Every tenth and twenty-fifth of the month, transfer the total amount in the **Income** account to the other accounts based on your CAPs. If you had $15,000 in commission deposits for the past two weeks, you would transfer money like this:

Income *5615 → It had $15,000 and goes to $0 because all money is transferred to the **Profit**, **Owner Pay**, **Tax**, and **Business Expenses** accounts based on your percentages.

Profit 1% (TAP 5%) *4313 → $150 goes here.
Owner Pay 35% (TAP 50%) *2617 → $5,250 goes here.
Tax 1% (TAP 15%) *3861 → $150 goes here.
Business Expenses 63% (TAP 30%) *7632 → $9,450
  goes here.

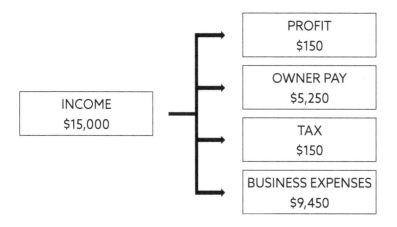

Step 3: You have $5,250 in your **Owner Pay** account to pay yourself. Only pay yourself based on your salary amount. If you pay yourself $2,000 twice a month, take $2,000 as owner pay and leave the remaining $3,250 in the **Owner Pay** account.

Step 4: You have $9,450 in your **Business Expenses** account to pay your bills. If you have $5,000 in expenses, pay those bills and leave the remaining $4,450 in the account.

Now your accounts will look like this:

Income *5615 → $0
Owner Pay 35% (TAP 50%) *2617 → $3,250
Business Expenses 63% (TAP 30%) *7632 → $4,450

Your out of sight, out of mind accounts will look like this:

Profit 1% (TAP 5%) *4313 → $150
Tax 1% (TAP 15%) *3861 → $150

Look at the percentages and amounts allocated to each of your accounts. What do you do if there isn't enough money to pay yourself, pay your taxes and cover your business bills? No, the correct answer is not "jump off a bridge." Nor is it to put a dunce cap on your pet lizard, George, and make him stand on one leg.

Before today, you may have spent most of your money if it was in the bank account. That solution didn't work. In addition to not getting ahead, you may have been filled with confusion about where all the money went. Now you have clarity on where the money goes. Soon, we'll adjust your percentages to move you closer to your target profitability.

Lack of money should be an alarm blaring that something is fundamentally broken in your business. You either do not earn enough or you spend too much—or maybe your business suffers from a combination of both. The Profit First system isn't the cause of your money problems. The business spends more money than it earns. See this for what it is: a warning. We'll use this warning to adjust your CAPs until your business becomes profitable.

Even if you can't pay everything on time, you need to stick to the system so you establish a healthy rhythm of cash flow. It may be a bit erratic now, but give it some time and continue to follow the system. Soon, your cash will flow in and out like the waves at the beach.

QUARTERLY BONUS

You've gotten through your first quarter. You changed directions and now control the money flow. It's time for your first profit bonus check. Yes, you read that correctly. You'll get cold, hard cash for all the effort you've made to improve your business. Remember the **Profit** account you set up at your out of sight, out of mind bank? For the past three months, you've diligently added money to it. Now it's time to reward yourself for running a profitable business.

This profit bonus is extra money you receive on top of the owner pay you take each month. Owner pay is what you get in return for all those hours you help people buy and sell their homes. The profit bonus is your reward for owning a profitable business. The only people who get a profit bonus are owners of the business.

On the first day of the new quarter, you get your profit bonus. Look at the balance in the **Profit** account and take 50%. If the account balance is $900, you get $450. Leave the other $450 in the account as part of your rainy-day fund. If you are the only owner, then you get the whole profit bonus. If there are multiple owners, you divide the $450 based on ownership percentages. If you own 40% of the company and your partner owns 60%, you would split the bonus up as follows:

Owner 1 (40% ownership) gets $180

Owner 2 (60% ownership) gets $270

How do you spend the profit? Any way you want. Get ten premium coffee drinks at your local specialty café, fill your belly at a Brazilian steakhouse, or take a nice vacation. You determine how you spend it.

Let me be clear on the one way you are not allowed to spend it: You cannot spend your profit on your business. The business already has enough, and it doesn't need your bonus. You need it. Don't fool yourself and say you will reinvest the profit bonus back into the business. If you reinvest the money, call it what it is: robbing yourself and your loved ones to overspend on business expenses. Show some leadership and spend on yourself instead of your business. Trust me, you will thank me for this later.

PAY THE TAX MAN

The **Tax** bank account is the other account at your out of sight, out of mind bank. Use the money in that account to pay your estimated quarterly taxes. If your accountant hasn't already told you what those estimated amounts should be, ask for them now. Every quarter, you'll take a bite out of your tax bill.

ADJUST YOUR PERCENTAGES

After you've taken your profit and paid your taxes, it's time to make adjustments. Every quarter, you will bump the percentages for your **Profit**, **Owner Pay** and **Tax** accounts and reduce the percentage that goes to your **Business Expenses** account. Consequently, you will allocate more of the money pie to yourself instead of the business.

You could adjust the CAPs by the same percentages you did when you went from Day Zero to Day One. Those adjustments were 1% to profit, 1% to owner pay, and 1% to tax. Consequently, you reduced business expenses by 3%. If that seems good enough for now, stick with that change. If you want to make larger adjustments, I suggest you read Chapter 9, where I give you tools and steps to review your progress and map out your adjustments for the next quarter.

You've set the profit wheel in motion. You should be excited, because you are moving in the right direction. As long as you continue to make progress each quarter, your business will make you more and more money. More of the money pie will belong to you. You'll keep more of what your business makes.

CHAPTER 7:

OPTIMIZE BUSINESS SPENDING

A few years ago, I took my wife and three children to Washington, DC. Since that trip, we added Zoe, our fourth child, to our lives. We went to the White House, the place I was most excited to see before the trip. My senator's aide, who sent me the tickets, told us that we would see Secret Service agents throughout the house and that they were a fountain of knowledge. One of the comments she made was, "You should brainstorm some questions to see if you can stump them." I shared the aide's challenge with my children. My then six-year-old daughter Claire came up with the best question: "Why is the White House white?" The agent responded that it was white because it was first painted with a limestone-based whitewash to protect the porous stone from freezing. Wow. The White House got its name from its paint color. Sometimes life can be so simple.

After our visit to the White House, we went to what turned out to be my favorite spot on the trip: The Bureau of Engraving and Printing. As we walked into the lobby, we saw an aluminum sign with a legend in black lettering, surrounded by dollar signs: "One Million Dollars in ten dollar notes." My mind quickly did the math: *One hundred thousand slips of paper.* All those bills were neatly stacked in a block surrounded by a glass case. *If I took the stack home with me, I'd be a millionaire.* Then I saw a gray placard at the bottom of the box with the words, "This exhibit is alarmed." *Guess I better come up with a different plan.*

"What would you do with all that money?" I asked my daughter Norah, who was seven at the time.

"I would go on a shopping spree at the American Girl doll store in Chicago. It's the biggest American Girl store in the world. They have a café where you can have lunch with your doll."

"That sounds like so much fun! What would you do with your money, Claire?"

"I'd buy all the Legos in the world. I would get the Friends Ferris Wheel and the roller coaster and the mansion. Eee!"

I chuckled and said, "We'd have to get you a bigger room to store all those Legos."

"Ya, I know, but we'd have a million dollars, so we could afford it."

"Maybe. It depends on how many Legos you buy."

Then I thought to myself, *Ah… this is how I got suckered by my child into making Lego the biggest toy company in the world.*

We all beamed as we fantasized about newfound wealth. We waited about a half an hour for our tour to start, and then it was our time to see how money gets made. We walked along a corridor about thirty feet above the factory floor. Below us, one of the workers grabbed a couple sheets of uncut currency.

He fanned his face with the paper as he said, "This is hard work!"

My children and I giggled. I thought, *I want to have his hard work.* At the end of the tour, I reflected on all the machinery and equipment. Raw materials went into the printing press. A plate applied 20,000 pounds of pressure per square inch to the paper and ink. Then a cutting machine sliced the sheets up into bills. *What would it be like to print money at will?*

You own a legal money-printing machine. With your business, you have the ability to create money from nothing. You can make as much money as you want. We would be foolish with our money press if we took some of the paper and lit it on fire or dumped the bottle of ink down the toilet. That would be pure stupidity. If we wanted the greatest amount of money possible for us to create, we would use every scrap of paper and drop of ink to print as much money as possible.

We would never throw away the raw ingredients. Why do we do so with our businesses? Why do we allow ourselves to waste money on expenses that do not add enough value?

How do we waste money? We sign up for services we don't use. We buy new products to replace old products we never used. We allow underperforming employees to continue to work for us because we are too conflict-averse to keep them accountable or introduce them to their next employer.

HOLD YOUR MONEY ACCOUNTABLE

I have often heard it said that money is the lifeblood of a business. Mike Michalowicz emphasizes this in *Profit First*.[18] Without money, you run out of business. Without money, your business dies quickly. In a profitable business, all the cash your business needs will come from your clients. Without profit, you must beg and borrow to pay your bills. Have you ever loaned your business money? Have you ever run up your credit card to cover those pesky bills?

Tom and I sat around my conference room table. He had just closed the biggest deal of his career, a whopping six-figure commission check for selling a multimillion-dollar home. That's more than most agents make all year. Everything should have

---

[18] Michalowicz, *Profit First*.

been rosy for Tom. Many real estate agents would be happy with a six-figure year. However, all was not well in his world.

I looked down at some reports I had prepared and said, "I reviewed your records. Your business expenses are $60,000 a month. What does your pipeline look like?"

"Four transactions are planned to close in October. That'll be forty grand GCI for October."

"What does November look like?"

"We've got $20,000 in commissions coming in for that month."

"Okay, $60,000 in business expenses and at best you've got $40,000 in commission lined up for next month. Where will the missing $20,000 come from?"

He shrugged his shoulders.

"You don't have enough commissions coming in to maintain these expenses. You simply cannot afford it. Last month, you spent $15,000 on internet ads. Over the past twelve months, how many of your home sales came from internet advertising?"

"Only three."

"You spent six figures on internet advertising. Only three of your home sales, worth $65,000, came from internet advertising. Does it make sense to spend $100,000 to make $65,000?"

"Three years ago, when I had my best year, most of my leads came from internet advertising," Tom protested. "I need to invest in advertising or all my business will dry up."

"But it's not working now. Internet advertising does not produce enough results for you to continue to spend at your current level."

"But it's worked in the past. I need people to see my name when they search the internet for a real estate agent."

Tom left our meeting confident that internet advertising would produce the results he wanted.

Eight months later, he called me. "Damon, I can't make payroll. I've spent the last year robbing Peter to pay Paul, and now Peter's dead. I don't know where to get the money. The only option I have is to pull money from my 401(k)."

"What does your pipeline look like?"

"It's not good. We only have six houses lined up for next month and four lined up for the following month."

"Eight months ago, you signed a contract with me to keep your money accountable, agreeing that you wouldn't spend more than you earned. You didn't adjust your spending below your earnings. Consequently, Peter suffocated. You must cut your expenses now. If you don't cut them now, you will need to pull $100,000 out of your 401(k) to cover payroll for the next three months. You have no other option."

"You're right, Damon. I'll cut my expenses," Tom said as he hung up the phone.

It saddened me to hear the frustration in Tom's voice. He'd had great success with those internet ads. They were the source of his best year. Why didn't they work now? He was convinced that internet ads would fill his sales pipeline again, so he continued to spend money on something that didn't work anymore. He'd had previous success with it and wanted to repeat those results.

We work so hard for sales. We don't want to reinvent the wheel every year. Tom's problem was, he kept his faith in something that no longer worked. His reliance on a faulty foundation put his business in peril.

BUSINESSES SHOULD HAVE ZERO EXPENSES

If you truly recognized the creative ability inherent in your business, you would strive to eliminate all your business expenses. Yes, you read that right.

"But Damon," you may think, "how am I supposed to operate my business without spending any money?"

I didn't say eliminate spending. I said eliminate all *expenses*. In other words, invest, don't spend. When you invest, you create new money. When you spend on expenses, you deplete your money. If you spend a dollar on advertising and it brings in one hundred dollars' worth of new business, did you spend money? No, you invested it.

When you invest money, you multiply it. If you spend $50,000 on an employee and consequently create $200,000 in income, did you spend it on the employee? No, you invested it and got a return on your money. What happens if you cut that $50,000 employee? You will lose $150,000 in profit.

Don't misunderstand me. You cannot spend your way to success in business. You can only invest your way to success. Your primary responsibility is to ensure that your business (a.k.a., money-printing press) operates at peak effectiveness and efficiency. You are the CAO—Chief Accountability Officer. If you don't keep your business and everything in it accountable, it will begin to stagnate and wither away.

When you invest, you should receive a return greater than the initial amount spent. It's not enough to invest a dollar and get one back. You get the same return with money in the bank, only with zero risk. That is a waste of opportunity. Whenever we choose one thing, we give up another.

The technical term for this situation is opportunity cost. Opportunity cost was my favorite business phrase during my second year of college, when my professor assigned me a short presentation on an economic term. I explained what opportunity cost was and shared the following example: I was a full-time student. When I chose to attend college, I also chose to not work full-time. To calculate the true cost of my education, I included the opportunity cost in the financial costs of attending the university.

My tuition was $1,200 per semester. When I started college, I had just ended my enlistment in the army, where I earned $1,200 per month. The true cost for me to attend one semester of college was the tuition ($1,200) plus the opportunity cost of four months of lost earnings (4 × $1,200). Taken together, tuition at $1,200 and opportunity cost at $4,800, my total cost for a semester of college was $6,000.

When we factor in opportunity cost, we gain a broader picture of the consequences of our decisions. When I choose to invest in one thing, it means I cannot invest in something else. I have limited resources. I owe it to myself to make the best investments possible.

Remove the word "expense" from your vocabulary. You are now a business investor. Every time a dollar leaves your business, it must be an investment. If it doesn't multiply your money, your responsibility as the Chief Accountability Officer is to eliminate the expenditure. Put on your big adult pants and show your cash who's boss.

How do you know if you are making an investment versus spending money on expenses? The first step is to follow the money. Too often, we squander resources because we allow ourselves to be distracted by the newest shiny object. You attend a webinar and learn about a fantastical new way to market. It's "guaranteed" to get you a thousand new leads. You spend money on the marketing tactic. The following month, you learn about another new marketing method "guaranteed" to get you ten thousand new leads. You try the new one for a month and then you learn about another new marketing method, one with fancy bells and silver whistles. If you look closely at this scenario, you will see Bonnie, The Distractor, as she tries to take you on another wild ride.

Does any of this sound familiar? Bonnie has billions of furry friends to help catch you in her snare. She may resort to dressing them up. How many times have you been caught up chasing those gold-sequined jacket-wearing squirrels? They giggle as they entice you. Meanwhile, Clyde pulls out a red and white-striped straw and, with puckered lips, sucks your bank account dry. Don't fall prey to the squirrels. Your brain weighs about 225 times more than the brain of one of those tree rats; I suspect that you are at least two times smarter than those devious rodents—unless you let the squirrels think for you. If you let the squirrels hijack your brain, you might as well put on a gold-sequined jacket and gather nuts for the rest of the year. I believe you're better than that.

Reframe the way you think about your spending now and for the rest of your life. Invest your resources so they have the highest possible return on investment (ROI). We all have limited resources. We have limited time. We have limited energy. We have limited money. Let's strive to multiply what we have so we enjoy our lives as much as possible and enrich the lives of our families, our communities, our nations, and the world. We want to be productive members of society and give more than we get.

Steve Prefontaine, the astounding Olympic runner, said, "To give anything less than your best is to sacrifice the gift."[19]

Everything we have is a gift, including our problems. They are opportunities. Think about one of your failures. What was a gift you received from it? There was an opportunity cost to your failure. You could have stayed in your comfort zone, but you chose a different path. You took a risk. Sometimes you win

---

[19] "Steve Prefontaine Quotes," BrainyQuote.com, accessed October 17, 2021, https://www.brainyquote.com/quotes/steve_prefontaine_109446.

when you take a risk. Other times, you lose. Look at your current resources. Multiply them into something much greater than they currently are. Don't fritter away your time, money, energy, and other resources. Invest them so they become increasingly and continuously more valuable.

HOW TO MEASURE RETURN ON INVESTMENT

When I make an investment, I look at my return in terms of time, money, or a combination of both. The investment must make me money. This is a pretty clear-cut measure. Either it makes me money, or it does not. When I use money on one thing, I say no to a bunch of other things. If I have ten dollars in my pocket and decide to buy a hamburger for ten dollars, I lose the opportunity to spend it on a chicken sandwich. When the money's gone, it's gone. How do we know if we make money? We measure it. I measure my return in two ways: payback and the rate of return.

PAYBACK

The payback determines how long it will take me to make back the money I invested. The shorter the payback, the better. I'm more interested in the return of my money than multiplying it. Some of my most profitable investments have been in professional education. I gain new skills to serve my clients better or in new ways.

Once, I invested $4,000 in a professional program. My target was to earn an additional $4,000 within three months. Any money I made beyond that original target was a bonus, a.k.a. a return. It was a good investment. At the end of three months, I had made $19,000. The payback period of three months became one of my investing benchmarks. I always ask myself how long it will take me to make back my original investment. If I can reasonably calculate a payback period of less than three months, I almost always move forward. You can use any time period you want to determine your payback period: years, months, days, seconds. I usually look at payback period in months.

RATE OF RETURN

With the rate of return, I look at how much I receive from the investment. I measure the return in a dollar amount and the percentage of the return. For example: I invest $1,000 in "just sold" postcards to mail to my prospect database. Someone signs a listing contract with me as a result and I earn a $3,000 commission. The return from the postcards is $2,000, the difference between my commission and the postcard cost. My return percentage is 200% ($2,000 return ÷ $1,000 investment).

You always want your return to be greater than 100%. If it isn't more than 100%, look for something else. You are better off not putting your money at risk. Consider the time and hassle you incur before you take the plunge. If I get a good return but it takes me too much time and hassle, I'd be wise to search for something else.

A year ago, one of my clients, Ernest, rented out his vacation home in the mountains. He called to tell me about it. "The mountain home has been a money pit. We spent all this money on furniture and doodads. Then we have to replace things because the renters don't respect our stuff. My wife and I are tired of renting out the mountain home. I don't think it's worth the hassle."

"That stinks," I said. "What will you do with the home?"

"I think we'll use it as we intended—as a vacation home. We enjoy our times in the mountains. It will be a relief to know if something breaks that we have nobody to blame but ourselves."

"That makes sense. What else is new?"

"My neighbor, Jasmine, just bought a beach home. She's killing it with her vacation rentals. She makes $4,000 a week. Are there any special tax advantages if I get another rental property?"

"You just told me you wanted to stop renting out the mountain house, and now you want buy a beach home. How much hassle was it to rent out the mountain home?"

"Quite a bit."

"Do you think it will be different with the beach home?"

"I'm not sure," Ernest replied. "I enjoy the mountains, and my wife Tameka loves running her toes through the sand at beach."

"Your neighbor says she makes a lot of rent money. Do you have all the details? How much hassle does she deal with? Does her beach home make a profit? You two are so busy with your jobs and children. Is it worth the extra hassle of a new rental property to make some extra money?"

"I don't know. I guess that's why I called you."

"Let's talk about the numbers and figure out how much you can make each year."

"I expect to rent the beach house out for $30,000 each year. I'll spend about $25,000."

"You'll keep $5,000 a year with the beach home. Assume you have the same amount of hassle with the beach home as you had with the mountain home. Is $5,000 enough to compensate you for the hassle?"

"But what about the tax benefits?" Ernest protested.

"Let's ignore the tax benefits right now," I told him. "First, you need to determine if the property is a good business decision. If it's not a good decision, the tax benefits don't matter. If it is a good decision, the tax benefits are gravy."

"Damon, $5,000 isn't enough money. It would be better for me to spend my time with referral partners. If I did that, I would sell three more houses this year, which would be worth a lot more than the money I'd potentially get from the beach rental."

"Makes sense."

One of the biggest benefits my clients get when we talk is, I slow down the conversation. We take a step back and determine the important factors in the situation. We put emotions in one bucket and logic in another. We start with the logic bucket and run the numbers. Do they make sense? Once we empty the logic bucket, we sift through the emotions and remove the excitement and fear from the scenario. How do you feel about it? Does it get you excited? Does it confuse you? Does it freak you out?

Whenever someone builds a house, they have a blueprint. The blueprint defines what materials are needed, how much, and where they go. Would you trust a contractor who builds a house without a blueprint? Of course not. When you transform your expenses into investments, you need a plan to give you the best results. With Profit First, you create a plan that gives you the same kind of power and control a general contractor has with a blueprint that ensures they can build a house that will last for decades.

It is better to run the numbers on paper to see if they work before you let go of a single dollar. Wouldn't you rather waste a piece of paper to realize you have a stinker than your precious money? If the numbers don't work on paper, rejoice: you've saved yourself a lot of heartache.

When you consider an investment, be conservative. It will typically costs twice as much as originally planned and take twice as long to create the desired return. Plan for a worst-case scenario. Don't speculate. Invest. When you run your numbers, use a lower-than-expected income amount. When you calculate your expenses, estimate a higher amount. If it still works with lower income and higher expenses, there is a better chance you will get a positive return from it.

MEASURE YOUR USE OF MONEY

One of the biggest expenses most real agents incur is in lead generation. How would your business change if you never wasted money on marketing again? How many more homes would you sell if all your marketing dollars got a positive return? It would almost be like you had a legal money-printing press. Imagine that. Here's the good news: Calculating your marketing return is a simple and easy process if you have the right system, which I share below.

The first step toward zero expenses is to measure how you use your money, so you will set up a return on investment (ROI) tracking system. This system shows you what your return is, and where you get the best return? Would it help to know where you get the best return? Armed with the data, you will make better decisions. Compare the commission you earn with the money invested to close the deal. Look at your last five buy and sell transactions. For each house, collect the following data:

- Address
- Source of client—how you got the client, whether via social media, internet advertising, sphere of influence, etc.

		Net		Cost of		
Address	Lead Source	Commission	Marketing	Sales	Return	ROI

TABLE 21: ROI TRACKING

- Net commission—the amount deposited into your bank account
- Marketing spend—the amount you spent to get the client
- Cost of sales—this includes money spent on signs, advertising, closing gifts, etc.

Fill in an ROI tracking table like Table 21 for the last five homes you sold.

Once you've entered the data for each property, calculate the return in dollar amount and percentage. For 123 Main Street, the return is $4,450 (Net Commission $5,000 − Marketing $50 − Cost of Sales $500).

Divide the return by the investment to calculate the percentage return. The return is $4,450. The total investment is $550 (Marketing $50 + Cost of Sales $500). The return on investment percentage is 809% (Return $4,450 ÷ Investment $550).

Look at the ROI tracking table and ask the following question: Which lead source gives the best return on investment? The

		Net		Cost of		
Address	Lead Source	Commission	Marketing	Sales	Return	ROI
123 Main	Sphere of Influence	$5,000	$50	$500	$4,450	809%
2 Maple	Social Media Ads	$3,000	$200	$300	$2,500	500%
Rogers	Event	$10,000	$1,000	$550	$8,450	545%
College	Internet Ads	$9,000	$1,591	$490	$6,919	332%
Lundee	Sphere of Influence	$4,500	$0	$600	$3,900	650%

sphere of influence provides the best return with 123 Main at 809% and 6 Lundee at 650%. The house at 2 Maple had the lowest return at 500%. Would you rather have an 809% or 500% return? With the 809% return, you get eight dollars for every dollar you invest. With 2 Maple, you only get five.

With this data, I adjust my marketing. I shift some of my social media spending to sphere of influence. I'd rather get eight dollars instead of five. With this shift, I superpower my money to multiply itself more.

It's important to keep your ROI tracking table current. The return you get from each source will fluctuate over time. Maybe next year, you'll get a better return with events. In eighteen months, you might make more with internet advertising. By keeping the table up-to-date, you'll discover trends and determine when it's time to redirect your funds.

Focus on improving your return on lead generation for the next few months. Improving your return on investment will give you a bigger bang for your buck than most other expenses.

The skills you develop to understand and improve your return will be valuable as you transition to the other expenses in your business.

Remember, you want a return greater than 100% or you burn money. Don't fall into the false thinking that you need to spend money on this or that. It's not how much you make that's important; it's how much you keep. The best thing you can do now to become a successful, profitable business owner is keep yourself accountable with your business expenses. Keep them within an appropriate percentage of your business income. If your business expenses percentage takes too much of your money pie, you have a shaky foundation and your business will collapse into itself as it grows.

If you have issues making ends meet at your current production level, those issues will magnify as your business grows. The pain and suffering from an unprofitable business will grow as you add more zeros to your gross commission income. Once you reach your work capacity, you'll run out of time. To grow, you will have to hire a contractor or employee, and then you will have to share some of your GCI with them. With each new transaction, you will keep less than you did before you tapped out your capacity. You may experience cognitive dissonance as a result. You may think, *I'm doing everything right. I'm growing my business through increased transactions, yet I'm getting further and further behind.* It's a distressing situation you can avoid now by getting your numbers right today.

DON'T THROW YOUR MONEY IN A BONFIRE

Let's discuss cutting fat from our businesses. We want to reduce nonperforming expenses. Too many vendors promise the moon and then underdeliver. When their system doesn't work, money is wasted. In such situations, one would be better off throwing their money into a bonfire. At least then they would see a show.

The key to minimizing waste is to stay accountable with your money. Develop a target return on investment and then measure your results from your investment against the target.

I've hired people on several occasions, both as employees and independent contractors. When I hire someone, I do it to make my job easier or to help me make more money. When someone doesn't add the right value to my company, they are not a good fit. Circumstances change, and what was once a good business relationship may no longer be beneficial. It's my job as the Chief Accountability Officer to make the necessary changes. Otherwise, I take money out of my children's mouths and give it to someone who doesn't do the job I hired them to do.

I hate burning money. I take responsibility every time I do it; I'm the one who lit the match. I can't do anything about the burnt money. It's long since been vaporized. No need to cry over it. However, I don't need to shovel more of my hard-earned money into the bonfire. I have complete control over my future spending and saving.

The return on investment you need to be profitable will most likely be higher than you initially think. When you fully understand the Profit First for Real Estate Agents system, you'll recognize that only a portion of each dollar your business earns belongs to you. Remember the money pie from Chapter 3? The concept of the money pie is we slice up our monthly income to cover the spending categories of owner pay, profit, tax, and business expenses.

The money pie showed us that our money is in the owner pay and profit slices. Focusing on the percentage of money you keep raises the bar for your return percentage. When you spend money on something, you eliminate the option to spend it on something else. If you incur a business expense, you divert that money from yourself.

Let me show you what I'm talking about.

You invest $1,000 in a direct mail campaign. You earn a $1,200 return from it. That sounds good, but as you'll see, you actually lose money. When we run the numbers to calculate how much money comes back into your pocket, you only get $600 because you have a 50% commission split with your buyer's agent. You lost $400. You need to earn more to get your money back.

To determine the ROI we need from our direct mail campaign, focus on the percentage the owner gets. We'll assume the owner pay percentage is 50% and profit is 5%, for a total of 55%. For every $1,000 the business earns, the owner gets $550. This means our direct mail needs to earn at least $3,636 before we breakeven on campaign. Every investment should create this kind of return, or it loses us money. We run successful companies. We need to avoid losing money as if the phenomenon were a zombie trying to chomp on our arm and turn us into the walking dead.

When you chase commissions without considering their profitability, you might enter a losing proposition. It's frustrating to see new money come in but then get eaten up, with nothing to show for your hard work. That's why you need to know your numbers.

TWO SIDES OF THE PROFIT COIN

Think about the humble copper penny for a moment. On one side we see the face of Abraham Lincoln. On the other side we see the Lincoln Memorial. In business, we have a profit coin with two sides. One side is revenues, and the other is expenses.

There are two ways to improve profits: increase revenue or decrease expenses. Often, when businesses struggle with money, it is because business expenses eat up too much of the income. The first step toward increasing profitability is to reduce the business expenses percentage. Assume a business spends 52% of its income on business expenses. In this scenario, $5,200 of a $10,000 commission goes to expenses. You keep $4,800. Less than half. You'd give yourself a $1,200 raise if you reduced your business expenses percentage to 40%.

Every business spends money on items that do not add enough value to justify the expenditure. It's time to identify areas where you can improve your financial discipline. Use the following one-week plan to improve your profit percentage:

Day 1: Print your bank and credit card statements for the last month.

Day 2: Grab a highlighter, review your statements, and highlight any items you think you could do without.

Day 3: Make a list of all the items you highlighted and include the following details: vendor name, expense type, and amount.

Day 4: Total the list of your highlighted expenses.

Day 5: Cut one expense from your list.

Day 6: Cut one more expense from your list.

Some people may find it difficult to cut expenses. Too often, when they bump against something difficult, they quit and return to what is "comfortable." You may experience some pain as you improve your business. It's part of the process. You will also experience pain if you don't choose to improve your business. The temporary pain of changing now will be short-lived and lead to better results. If you choose to delay and put change off till tomorrow, you'll avoid the pain now—but the problems will continue to fester, and you'll experience greater pain over a longer period of time. Which pain will you choose, short-term or long-term?

The most important thing for you to do now is act. You don't have to cure cancer. You just need to start. If you read this book and simply place it on a shelf to gather dust, it will not serve you. If you cut one expense now, you will have made money from this book. The first step toward progress is to take one step. As you take one step, it will lead you to another. I've just given you six steps toward improving your profit percentage. These steps are small, actionable tasks so you can complete each one in less than ten minutes.

Improving your finances is a major undertaking. It will take some time to achieve the results you desire. Your profits don't have to be ideal tomorrow. My goal is to help you take a small step each day. Each step will multiply your profits over time.

Let's say you currently spend 52% of your net commission income on business expenses. Assume your target business expenses percentage is 40%. You determine that you want to improve your profits by 12% over the next twelve months. If you reduce business expenses by 1% each month, you will achieve your profit goal.

Assume your current business expenses are $17,333 per month. To get to your target business expenses percentage, you need to reduce your expenses by $2,079. That may seem like a lot. What if we split the amount into smaller bites? We have twelve months to make our improvements, so if we reduce our expenses by $173 each month, we will hit our profitability goal. Which seems easier, $2,079 or $173?

Another way to improve profits is to increase commission income and keep business expenses the same. If your average commission is $7,000, increase the average commission. This can be done by increasing the commission rate you charge or the price of the houses you sell, or both.

You have multiple ways to get to your target business expenses percentage. Use your creative brain to arrive at your new business expenses target. One way that Bonnie, The Distractor, foils you is by chopping away at your self-confidence. She'll kick you in the ribs when you're lying on the ground with a bloody lip from the last deal that went south. Then she'll kneel down and whisper in your ear, "Oh you can't do that. It's too difficult." When you hear her mischievous voice, ask the following question:

How *can* I do it?

Ask this question over and over again until your brain devises different solutions to your overspending on business expenses.

CUTTING FAT VS. CUTTING MUSCLE

When we adjust our target business expenses, it can be easy to throw the baby out with the bathwater. The need to cut expenses doesn't mean the expenses have zero benefits. We want to get rid of expenses, not investments.

To make this clearer, I'll call expenses fat and investments muscle. Investments in your business should create more money for you. When you spend one dollar on an investment, it needs to provide you with a return greater than one dollar. Here's an example: You make a $1,000 investment in a marketing method, which leads to a new home transaction that earns you a $10,000 commission. Next month, you invest the same $1,000 and get another home transaction that pays you a commission of $10,000.

Over a few months, you get consistent results. You have an investment that gives you a 10x return every time. This is a good example of muscle in the business. Continue to make the investment. Increase your investment to see if you can continue to get a 10x return. What if you made a $2,000 investment and got $20,000 from two home transactions that month? That is a great marketing system. Continue to feed it as long as you get an appropriate return.

When you know the ROI of each of your investments, you can shift your spending from lower performers to higher ones. This takes time, and you have to measure your results; but as you can see, you get some significant profitability gains when you devote more of your resources toward better-performing investments.

TRANSFORM EXPENSES INTO INVESTMENTS

Once you understand the measuring stick for expenses and investments, it's time to transform each of your expenses into investments. When you do this, you transform a cash drain into something that prints money. Which would you rather have?

This all sounds great, but where do you start? Choose one expense to convert at a time. When you focus on one expense at a time, you will see much better results than you will if you try to change everything at once.

The first step is to look at your list of expense categories. Determine how significant each of these categories is to your business by dividing the total category expenses by your net commission income. This will tell you how large the expense is as a percentage of net commission income. Ask yourself what your current return on investment is for the category of expenses. Then write down your return on investment percentage for each.

The next step is to review each expense category and ask the following question: What can I do to get a better return on my investment for this category of expenses? Write down at least three answers for this question for each category of expenses. For example: You spend twenty dollars on lunch every day. How could you turn your lunch money into more money? One way would be to take a referral partner out to lunch. What are some other ways?

Continue the process until you have three ways to improve your ROI for each expense category. Now it's time to prioritize your ROI improvement ideas. You will rank them in the following three ways:

- Easy
- Quick
- Profitable

Rank how easy the idea is to implement from 1–5. 1 is hard to implement and 5 is easy to implement. In this ranking system, you cannot use the number 3. Removing 3 from the ranking system forces you to decide: it is either hard or easy. Here are your ranking numbers: 1, 2, 4, 5.

Once you've ranked your ROI improvement ideas, it's time to make a list of the ideas you will implement over the next ninety days. Choose the easiest idea to implement, the quickest idea to implement, and the most profitable idea to implement.

Easiest to implement: Sort your list based on what is easiest to implement, 5 being the easiest. Now choose one of the easiest ideas to work on over the next ninety days.

Quickest to implement: Sort your list based on what is quickest to implement, 5 being the quickest. Now choose one of the quickest ideas to work on during the next ninety days.

Most profitable to implement: Sort your list based on what is most profitable to implement, 5 being the most profitable. Choose one of the most profitable ideas to work on for the next ninety days.

You've narrowed your list down to the most profitable, quickest, and easiest ideas. Order these three ideas—which one will you implement first? Second? Third?

You have your marching orders for the next ninety days. Put blinders on and work on the first idea until you've implemented it. Once you've finished with your first idea, move on to the second. Once you finish your second, work on the third idea.

Write down all the things you must do to accomplish idea number one. Slice the elephant into small, bite-sized pieces. You'll gain clarity on the work you need to do to complete this activity. Then make a list of all the steps you must complete to accomplish ideas two and three.

You now have an action plan for each of your top three profitable ideas. There should be no question in your mind about what you need to do to turn three of your expenses into investments over the next ninety days. If there is any doubt, now is the time to fill in the gaps. You need complete clarity in your action plan. Without complete clarity, you will run into roadblocks that will slow you down and keep you from enjoying a bank account that is flush with cash.

Work on one idea at a time. Focused energy yields better results than trying to tackle all three items at once. Your goal should be to complete your number one idea within the next ninety days.

CHAPTER 8:

SUPERCHARGE YOUR PROFITS

Several years ago, I attended a conference. The main topic of conversation was monthly revenue production. I attended the conference because I wanted to grow my business. George, another attendee, told me that his annual business revenue was almost $2 million. As we talked, I learned that his owner compensation, paid in salary and distributions, was around $150,000 that year. Something about this didn't compute.

George had a staff of ten. He spent a significant amount of money on marketing. As he talked, the wheels in my brain spun faster and faster. I was bewildered. That year, my revenues were around $300,000. Yet I had a staff of just one: me. My owner compensation was around $150,000. While George and I had different revenues, we were paid the same amount as owners. Did it make sense to grow my business by seven times and obtain the same owner compensation as George? Why would I want to make all the investments to grow and not make any more money?

Profit is a better indicator of business success than your gross commission income. Don't focus on how much money your business makes. Focus on how much your business keeps.

What do you want to achieve with your business? What's important for you? You don't need to compete with anyone. Too often, people get caught up in the hype of their peer groups. They want to measure up and be the best of the best. You don't need to be better than someone else. You only need to be the best version of yourself.

Few people have defined what they want from their business. Why not? It takes time, thought, and work to gain clarity on what is important, but when people don't take the time to develop their own definitions of success, they become prisoners to others' dreams and aspirations. They waste valuable time, money, and resources as they reach for the next rung on someone else's ladder of success. When they arrive at the top of the ladder, they are drained. *Was it all worth it?* they think. No, because they didn't work on what was important to them.

It's important to define what success looks like for you. Work on what is important to you. Don't work on what someone else perceives as cool or exciting. If it's not meaningful to you, then achieving it won't improve your life.

When I was a teenager, my mother asked me, "If everyone else were to jump of a cliff, would you?" Should your goal be $1 million GCI just because your friend Sally has that goal? What about your circumstances is the same as your friend Sally's? What about your circumstances is different? What price will she pay to achieve her $1 million GCI goal? Will you pay the same price?

I'm not saying you should or shouldn't strive for a $1 million GCI, or any other goal. Strive for what is important to you. Does it make sense to work on something that is insignificant to you? If you want to work for someone else's dream, get a job.

In this chapter, we focus on the income side of the profit coin. You'll learn how to make your home sales more lucrative.

PRICING

For most businesses, pricing is a complex subject. However, pricing for real estate agents is simple. Your commission is a percentage of the sales price of the house. Let's review pricing based on your average commission earned for a transaction.

What is your average commission? Look at your 1099 from last year and divide it by last year's total transactions. Here's an example: You made $144,900 on your 1099 and sold thirty-four homes. Your average commission was $4,262.

Your commission is based on two variables: commission percentage and house price.

Ask yourself:

- What commission rate do I charge?
- What is the price range of the houses I sell?

Look at the last year to collect data on commissions you received for houses you sold. Then create a list of all the home sales you made in the last twelve months. In another column, write down the commission you received on each sale.

Total the gross commission you received for each transaction to get your total gross commission income for the last twelve months. Divide your total gross commission income by the number of transactions to get your average commission per transaction.

For example, let's say you received commissions totaling $129,200 for twenty-three houses. Your average commission is $5,617. We'll use your average commission per transaction to calculate your margin per house. I'll give you a new measurement you can use to leverage your time and create more profits.

MARGIN

Margin is the most important factor in your average transaction. I've said it before, and I'll say it again: It doesn't matter how much you make; it matters how much you keep.

Scenario 1: You get a $10,000 commission on a house.

Scenario 2: You get a $6,000 commission on a house.

Which commission would you prefer?

The costs for the Scenario 1 transaction total $6,000. You keep $4,000 of the commission.

The costs for the Scenario 2 transaction total $1,000. You keep $5,000 of the commission.

Which commission would you prefer?

Now let's factor in the time it takes you to service the transaction, from soup to nuts.

In Scenario 1, you spend a total of ten hours on the house. How much do you make per hour in this scenario? A $4,000 commission divided by ten hours equals $400 per hour.

In Scenario 2, you spend a total of twenty hours on the house. How much do you make per hour in this scenario? A $5,000 commission divided by twenty hours equals $250 per hour.

You have a limited amount of time. Assume that you have 1,800 hours per year to work because you want to have a life. Assume that 80% of your time is available for activities related to closing transactions. You have 1,440 hours available to earn money. In Scenario 1, you earn $400 per hour. Your maximum earnings would be $576,000. In Scenario 2, your maximum earnings would be $360,000. Do you see now why margin is an important aspect to measure in your business?

When we initially looked at Scenarios 1 and 2, most people would have chosen Scenario 1 because the commission is higher. After you factor in the profit in both scenarios, most people would choose Scenario 2 because the profit is higher.

Next, we added some context and learned that the amount of money we earn per hour is $150 greater in Scenario 1.

When you focus only on number of transactions, you may have a misguided approach to growth. Dive deeper into your data so you can learn where to make improvements. This is why it makes sense to examine your data on a regular basis. What worked well last year may not work as well this year. Things change. Constantly monitor the important metrics in your business to see when a shift occurs. The sooner you recognize the shift, the sooner you'll adjust your approach. You'll be able to capitalize on the new opportunities that come with every such shift.

From now on, I want you to focus on the profit per hour you generate in your business. Your time is your most limited resource. You only get twenty-four hours a day, and when those twenty-four hours pass, they are gone forever. Time is the only asset you have that, once spent, cannot be replicated. Time is no respecter of people. Time is the great leveler.

CLONING BEST CLIENTS

A few years ago, I knew something was off in my business. I loved my clients, but I needed something different. I resisted change because life was amazing. I made good money. I had time off to enjoy with my family. I was in a comfort zone. I was so cozy, I became complacent and experienced some stagnation. I began to yearn for the energy of the early years, when I struggled to turn my dreams into reality. I wanted to get back in the fight again. I had to force myself out of my comfort zone. At times, the comfort zone reached out to me to bring me back, but I persisted outside the zone.

Then I read *Surge* by Mike Michalowicz. Consequently, I changed my business. The key message of *Surge* is to pick a niche and serve it. When you focus on a niche, you become an expert. In the book, Mike repeats a phrase that is common in the marketing world: "The riches are in the niches."[20] I decided to commit myself to a niche of clients.

Here's the process I went through to determine my ideal client.

I created a spreadsheet with the following columns:

- Client name
- Annual revenue amount
- Industry
- Likability factor (indicated by a smiley face or a frowny face)

I listed all my clients and added the annual revenue, industry, and likability factor data for each. Next, I sorted the list by annual revenue from highest to lowest. I looked at my list to interpret what it was telling me. Here is what I learned:

- About 20% of my clients were responsible for 80% of my revenue.
- The 20% of my clients responsible for 80% of my revenue were real estate agents.
- Each of the 20% had a smiley face in their likability factor column.
- The quickest-growing businesses were in real estate.

---

[20] Mike Michalowicz, *Surge: Time the Marketplace, Ride the Wave of Consumer Demand, and Become Your Industry's Big Kahuna* (Boonton, NJ: Obsidian Press, 2016).

Hmm. Maybe I should choose real estate agents as my niche. I had known for years that I enjoyed working with real estate agents. Now I had objective data. I mulled over the information for a week and then made a strategic declaration: I will focus on real estate agents.

Here are a few reasons why I like y'all: You are some of the most business-savvy people I've ever met. You have moxie. You are problem-solvers. You focus on growth. You want to become the best versions of yourselves. You make a difference.

Over the past ten years, I have become an integral part of my real estate agent clients' businesses. Many had struggled with their finances. I know how to deconstruct, demystify, and simplify the money side of their businesses, so I was able to help by making money easier to understand.

My new focus on agents made everything so much simpler. A huge weight was lifted from my shoulders. My main goal became to learn as much as I could about the industry so I could understand agents' specific money issues. Better understanding of their problems led me to develop valuable solutions.

People will always pay someone to solve their problems.

One of the most profitable things you can do for your business is to choose a niche to focus on. This is the best way to differentiate yourself from the sea of other agents in your local market. When you chose a niche, you gain leverage. You raise yourself up to become an expert in your chosen niche. The money and time you devote to your niche gets better results than general efforts. You get a better return for marketing dollars and more money in your pocket for the same amount of work. How does that sound to you?

"But Damon," you may say, "it was easy for you to choose a niche." It wasn't. When I started my business in 2008, my goal was to help small business owners with accounting and taxes because I knew they needed it. I wanted to help anyone who would hire me. A few people asked me who my ideal client was. I replied, "A small business owner." What a vague answer. I might as well have told them I was wanted to work with anyone who could fog a mirror.

When I ask agents who they want to help, the most common response I hear is that they want to help buyers or sellers. When I ask them who their ideal client is, the response is often "Anyone who wants to buy or sell a house." This is similar to the response I used for nine years—"I want to work with small business owners." In essence, I said I want to work with anyone who will pay me. The problem with this approach is, you must cast a very wide net to work with just anyone.

But how do you choose a niche? The best place to start is with your past clients. They are a goldmine of information. You formed a partnership with them to solve a problem of buying or selling their home. They trusted you. They paid you. You want to work with people who buy from you. People who will buy from you in the future are similar to people who have bought from you in the past.

It's your turn to start your journey to choose a niche. Use the same approach I did to find mine. You will need the following items:

- A list of your closed transactions for the last twelve months (if twelve months appears to be too much work, use a list from the last three months)
- Pen and paper or a spreadsheet on your computer

Create the following columns:

- Client name
- House address
- Type of transaction (buy/sell)

- Neighborhood
- Net commission—the amount of money deposited into your bank account
- Likeability factor—smiley face or frowny face
- Details

In the details section, write down the things you remember about your clients. Age, marital status, children, career, hobbies, etc. Write down as many details as you can.

Once you complete your list, look at it for a while. What do you notice? What do your clients have in common? Make notes about your observations. Sort your list based on the net commission you received. What do you observe when you look at it now?

Sort your list based on likability factor. What do the clients with the smiley face have in common? What do the clients with the frowny face have in common? Make notes about your observations. Look at all your notes.

If I move my focus from my best clients to the other 80% of my clients, I lose leverage. In my marketing and sales activities, I focus only on those who are similar to the 20% who are my best clents.

Why do I focus on the 20%?

- They are the ones I enjoy working with the most
- They are the ones I help the most
- They are my best and most profitable clients

Next, we will explore what I call an 80/20 activity. An 80/20 activity is one that will make a significant impact on your business or life.

What's the one thing that will have the biggest impact in an area of your business?

WORK SMARTER, NOT HARDER

A common misconception with Profit First is that it's all about reducing expenses. While lower expenses are an important component of the system, profitability is more than just cutting expenses. Abraham Maslow said, "I suppose it is tempting, if the only tool you have is a hammer, to treat everything as if it were a nail."[21] If we only increase profitability via cost reduction, we miss out on some of the more powerful profit improvement solutions.

The most powerful business concept ever invented is the Pareto principle. It was discovered by Vilfredo Pareto, who conducted a study: He observed that 80% of the wealth in society was held by 20% of the population.[22]

The Pareto principle is also known as the 80/20 rule. The 80/20 rule applies to many facets of people's businesses:

- 80% of sales come from 20% of clients
- 20% of time produces 80% of a business's income
- 20% of our work typically results in 80% of our success

Once you recognize and apply the Pareto principle in your business, you will get more results in less time, with fewer expenses and less effort. Additionally, you will recognize how important it is to focus your priorities on what gives you the best results. Do you work more hours than you should? How much time do you waste on busywork? Busywork is pernicious. It appears to be so important at the time, but is it? Sadly, most

---

[21] Abraham Maslow, *The Psychology of Science: A Reconnaissance* (New York, NY: HarperCollins, 1966).

[22] Britannica, T. Editors of Encyclopaedia. "Vilfredo Pareto." Encyclopedia Britannica, August 15, 2021. https://www.britannica.com/biography/Vilfredo-Pareto.

of us waste too much time on so-called urgent tasks that are actually unimportant and suck the life out of us.

Be intentional about every aspect of your business. Maximize your time, money, and resources. Don't squander your short life on this third rock from the sun.

Author Jim Rohn said, "Let others lead small lives, but not you. Let others argue over small things, but not you. Let others cry over small hurts, but not you. Let others leave their future in someone else's hands, but not you."[23]

While you are destined for greatness, it is your responsibility to go and grab it. Greatness will not come to you; you must choose it.

FOCUS YOUR MARKETING

When you develop your marketing, remember: You don't need to do everything. There are five million and one different ways to go about it, and you only have so much time, money, and energy. Don't spread yourself too thin. Choose—at most—three ways to market, and then ignore everything else. When Bonnie the squirrel approaches you, wearing a new firework-shooting jacket, look her directly in the eyes and shake your head. Then open your mouth and utter these words: "Go away, you nasty vermin!"

You don't need more than three marketing methods, because 80% of your business will come from one to three ways you put out the good word about yourself. "But what should I choose?" you may ask. "With so many options, how do I choose the best one?" Look at yourself for the answer. Look at how you marketed your business during the last twelve months, and you will learn the best method for you.

---

[23] "Jim Rohn Quotes," BrainyQuote.com, accessed October 17, 2021, https://www.brainyquote.com/quotes/jim_rohn_147504.

Remember the ROI tracking table (Table 21) we created in Chapter 5? You will now expand it for your marketing so you can make more money from your home sales this year. Expand the table to include all your transactions from the last twelve months.

It's time to calculate your return dollar amount and ROI percentage.

Step 1: Calculate your total return for each lead source by subtracting marketing and cost of sales from your net commission.

Step 2: Calculate the ROI percentage to see which lead source multiplies our investment the most.

If you only looked at the return amounts, you'd think events are the clear winner. However, when you look at the ROI percentages, you get a more complete answer.

When we look at the chart now, we see the best return comes from our sphere of influence. The return from sphere of influence was more than two times better than that from social media ads. Assuming ROI percentage remains the same, what would happen if we moved $1,000 of our social media ad money to sphere of influence?

Provided we spent the same amount of money on our marketing, it would increase our profits by more than $12,000.

When you focus your investments on fewer methods, you will get better results than you would with a scattershot approach. Decide which three methods you will invest in for the next three months. Anytime you are tempted by a new method, write it on a "Maybe Later" list for you to evaluate when you develop your action plan for next quarter.

As you keep track of your marketing investments, results, and returns on investment, you will gain valuable data. This data will guide you to make better decisions about how you should deploy your marketing dollars. Your goal should be to increase your marketing ROI each quarter. Incremental improvements in your marketing ROI will make your marketing money-printing machine more effective. You will multiply the money you make from your investments.

TABLE 23: LEAD SOURCES

ad Source	Net Commission	Marketing	Cost of Sales	Return	ROI
Events	$85,000	$9,000	$4,500	$71,500	530%
phere of nfluence	$35,000	$2,000	$2,000	$31,000	775%
cial Media Ads	$22,000	$5,000	$400	$16,600	307%
Total	$142,000	$16,000	$6,900	$119,100	520%

TABLE 24: IMPROVING LEAD SOURCES ROI

ad Source	Net Commission	Marketing	Cost of Sales	Return	ROI
Events	$85,000	$9,000	$4,500	$71,500	530%
phere of fluence	$52,500	$3,000	$3,000	$46,500	775%
cial Media Ads	$17,600	$4,000	$320	$13,00	307%
Total	$155,00	$16,000	$7,820	$131,280	551%

CHAPTER 9:

QUARTERLY CELEBRATION

I called up Abby, a successful real estate agent in Oklahoma.

"How are you, Abby?"

"Fantastic! Twenty-eight days ago, I was on the operating table. The doctors sliced my chest open and massaged my heart. A few hours earlier, I'd had a heart attack."

"Oh my goodness," I replied. They were the only words I could think to utter.

"I'm so happy to be alive. I can't believe all the stupid stuff I use to worry about. None of that garbage mattered."

"Wow!"

There was a zest in Abby's voice that I'd never heard before. I could feel him transmitting energy from his gigantic smile through his voice.

"My life started twenty-eight days ago. I lived a good life before, but now things are different. I have a new lease on life. I'll celebrate my life for the gift it is. If something doesn't bring me joy, it has no place in my life."

Abby's words touched my heart in a way very few words have. It wasn't just his words that impacted me. It was his energy. He had always had that energy inside him, but he had allowed stupid stuff to bog him down. Then he stared death in the face, lived to tell me about it, and took a new approach to life.

We don't need to have near-death experiences to learn the powerful lesson Abby learned (and taught me). Every year, each of us reach an important milestone—our birthdays. Some celebrate with cake and ice cream. Others ignore it as just another day. Each year, as I finish another trip around the sun, I reflect on the past 365 days. What did I learn? How am I different? What do I want the next twelve months to look like?

In Profit First, we throw a party every three months. I call it the Quarterly Celebration. We tally our wins, learn from our failures, and get a cash bonus. Doesn't that sound amazing?

Think of a way you can spend your profits in a way that celebrates your wins. It's time to enjoy the money you've worked so hard for. Do something you enjoy. You earn money so you can enjoy what it will buy you. If you're having difficulty thinking of something enjoyable, think back to what you enjoyed as a child or teenager. There is a good chance that if you enjoyed it in your youth, you will enjoy again.

Here are a few things I've spent my profit bonuses on:

- A vacation to Ireland
- Scuba diving certification, complete with all the diving gear
- Paying off personal credit card debt
- Building up my personal cash savings
- Fly fishing gear
- A vacation to Florida with my family
- Scuba diving certification for my daughter Claire so I can build memories with her

Profit First is a repeatable process in which you constantly improve your profits. In this chapter, you will learn the vital tasks to perform once each quarter to keep your business on track. Every quarter you will celebrate your successes, learn from your experiences, and set your objectives for the next three months.

WITHOUT TRACKING, YOU HAVE NO IDEA IF YOU'RE MAKING PROGRESS

Too often, in the day-to-day hustle and bustle of work, we become tangled in the weeds and lose track of what we want to accomplish. Do you feel like you constantly put out fires? Do you feel certain about how many transactions you will close next month? Do you know how much money you will make in the next twelve months?

If you answered yes to the first question and no to either or both of the second two, you might be running your business by the seat of your pants. If you don't know how you perform in each of these areas, you will wander without a clue. You'll be in reactive mode instead of proactive mode.

Track the important numbers of your business. Each of the following four areas should have a few key numbers that keep you informed about how successful you are.

- Sales/marketing
- Operations
- Financial
- Personal

The key numbers in your business are called metrics. A metric is something you measure.

I had the following conversation with my daughter Claire:

"How's the weather?" I asked.

"It's nice."

"What do you mean?"

"It's ninety-eight degrees. Humidity is 75%. Partly cloudy. Wind speed five miles per hour."

"That sounds nice. As soon as I walk outside, I'll be smack-dab in the middle of Dante's inferno. At least now I know what someone else thinks nice weather is."

When we use data to describe the weather, we get a clear picture of it. We have four data points: temperature, humidity, degree of cloudiness, and wind speed. Four data points and I know if I should wear shorts and a T-shirt and if I'll need to apply sunscreen. To collect these data points, I need the following tools: a thermometer, a hygrometer, an anemometer, and at least one functioning eyeball. Okay, maybe I'm a bit geeky or old-fashioned. I like technical gear. If you have a smartphone, you can probably get all this data from an app.

The ideal time period to use to plan for your business is three months. When you change your focus to improving your business in ninety-day sprints, you harness power for the following reasons:

- You have enough time to accomplish something significant
- The time is limited enough for you to maintain urgency and get things done by the end of the quarter
- You are forced to focus on only a few key objectives

Each quarter, I choose three things to improve in my business. One quarter, I chose the following:

- Improve monthly revenue by $6,000
- Establish a set sales process
- Set up and use a Customer Relations Management System

These three objectives guided the actions I took, week in and week out, throughout the quarter. They gave me a filter through which I could see what was most important for me to work on.

I ask myself a simple question when Bonnie, The Distractor, shows her cute, devious face and begs for my time, money, and attention: Does this help me accomplish one of my three quarterly objectives? If the answer is no, then I tell Bonnie to get lost.

After you choose your three quarterly objectives, focus on one at a time. When you focus on one thing, you will give it your best effort. You will accomplish more when you focus on one goal than if you split your focus between five, ten, or a hundred goals.

Track your actions and the results of those actions. If you only track your results, you won't identify the actions you took to achieve the results. On the other hand, if you only track your actions, you won't know that your work produced the desired results. When you track both, you gain valuable insight into what works, what doesn't work, and where to improve.

Several years ago, one of my clients, Julian, told me that he only works on something if he can measure it. He wants to know if the work he performs creates his desired results. He told me that if he can't measure something, he immediately says no to it. If he can't measure it, he doesn't know if it works or doesn't work. He doesn't want to fritter his life away on items that don't improve it. When we track our activities and their results, we gain objective data that will help us improve our businesses.

Continuous improvement over time will yield astounding results. Assume you improve your profits by 1% a week. Over the course of fifty-two weeks, you will improve your profits by 52%. If your business generates profit of $100,000 a year, your profit will be $152,000 a year from now. What would you do with an extra fifty-two grand?

It's easier to grow with small, incremental improvements than it is to grow with a few large changes. Work to become a master of small, incremental improvements. They will seal leaks in your money pipeline and keep your resources from dwindling.

Every three months, you will have a Quarterly Celebration in your business. As high achievers, we seldom take the time to celebrate our victories and reward ourselves for the work we do. We keep our noses to the grindstone until they are an ugly mess. We place demands on ourselves and minimize our heroic efforts. We treat ourselves much worse than we would allow anyone to treat our worst enemies. In many ways, we become our own worst enemy.

That stops now. From now on, you will reward yourself for the results you achieved during the previous three months. This is the process I call the Quarterly Celebration. It reinforces the behaviors you adopted to achieve success. You need positive reinforcement to buoy you when things get difficult. When you run into challenges, think about the party you'll have in less than three months. Who doesn't love a good party? Positive reinforcement strengthens the odds that you will maintain and improve what works in your business.

The Quarterly Celebration gives you objective, holistic data about the growth and health of your business. The four phases of the Quarterly Celebration are:

- Revisit
- Review
- Reap
- Reach

TABLE 25: REVISIT			
	Period _____	Day Zero CAPs	TAPs
Net Commission Income			
Profit			
Owner Pay			
Tax			
Business Expenses			

REVISIT

During the Revisit phase, you review each of the five slices of your money pie. Complete Table 25 based on your Day Zero CAPs. By revisiting your Day Zero CAPs, you can gauge how your business has grown.

Enter the actual amounts for net commission income, profit, owner pay, tax, and business expenses in the first column. Next, enter the CAPs for the first quarter you started Profit First for Real Estate Agents. Then enter the TAPs based on your net commission income amount when you started.

As you revisit where you came from, what stands out to you? What were your goals when you started your Profit First Rollout Plan? Write them down.

TABLE 26: REVIEW			
	Period _____	CAPs	TAPs
Real Revenue			
Profit			
Owner Pay			
Tax			
Business Expenses			

REVIEW

Now we move into the Review phase. In this phase, you review any changes you made during the last three months.

Enter the actual amounts for net commission income, profit, owner pay, tax, and business expenses in the first column of Table 26. Next, enter the CAPs for the prior quarter. Then enter the TAPs you used for that quarter.

What were your goals when you started last quarter? Assess your progress toward each of these goals. Ask yourself the following questions:

- Which goals did I accomplish?
- Which goals am I still working on?
- What do I need to do to reach my unmet goals?

Now that you've completed another quarter, what is your current perspective regarding Profit First?

REAP

Now we move into the fun part of the Quarterly Celebration—the Reap phase. Think of a farmer, growing his prize crop. He plows the ground and plants seeds. He sweats while he tends his crop beneath the hot summer sun. In the fall, the crop bursts with abundance, and he works to harvest the maximum yield.

Does the farmer cut down his crop and till it back into the soil so he can reinvest it for next year? No, of course not! The farmer reaps the crop. He needs food for his family and loved ones. The farmer devoted a whole year to the crop. The work he performed in spring and summer led to the harvest in the fall. The farmer relishes the fruits of his labor.

You must do the same thing in your business. You must reap money from it. During the Reap phase, you get some money! Shout for joy, clap your hands, and revel in your newfound profits and success. You get a bonus for all your hard work. Money is one of the best reinforcers of positive progress.

BONUS TIME

It's time for your quarterly profit distribution. Review your **Profit** bank account and write down the balance at the end of last month. If it is now July, look at your June bank statement. Divide the ending **Profit** bank account balance by two.

For example, say you have $1,296.38 in your **Profit** account. When you divide that number by two to calculate your bonus, you get $648.19. This is your bonus. Write yourself a profit bonus check and take a picture of yourself with it. Print the picture and hang it on your office wall to remind you that your business is set up to be permanently profitable. You may want to create a Profit Wall.

Every quarter, take a new picture with your latest profit bonus check and add it to your Profit Wall. A picture is worth a thousand words, and this visual record of your profit success will not only positively reinforce the improvements you make in your business, it will also reinforce *why* you're in business: to make a profit. You are in business to grow your bank accounts so you can live your ideal life.

Avoid the temptation to "reinvest" your profit back into your business. If you do, you need to call it what it is: spending on business expenses. Prior to Profit First, you may have lived with muddy financial waters. All your spending (profit, owner pay, tax, and business expenses) was comingled in one bank account. Now you have clarity about your finances. You use separate bank accounts to simplify and understand your money. Don't repeat your prior behavior and think you'll get a different result.

I would rather have you burn your profit distribution than "reinvest" it back into your business. You've already invested enough in your business; you don't need to pump more money into it. Enough is enough!

When you set up your Profit First for Real Estate Agents system, you created boundaries around your spending with the separate bank accounts. Don't cross your boundaries. Practice self-leadership. Show the business you are the boss. It's time to invest in yourself, your family, and your loved ones.

What will you do with the beautiful bundle of cash from your profit bonus? I suggest you have some fun. This is your money. What is something fun you want to do, buy, or share with someone? Imagine you found a forgotten twenty-dollar bill in your pocket. What would you do with it?

When I was eight years old, I lived in Berlin, Germany. Every afternoon, the ice cream truck would come to our neighborhood, and the speaker affixed to its roof would belt out the same joyous song to announce that heaven on earth had arrived. The world would stop as soon as I heard the music. I'd turn my head, beaming, and my mouth would begin to water as glee rose in my heart.

I'd bolt up the four flights of stairs to our apartment and ask, "Mom, can I have some ice cream money?"

She'd smile as she placed a few coins in my hand, and I'd run like the wind to catch the ice cream truck before the line of children disappeared.

My favorite ice cream flavor was lemon. I salivated when I imagined the delight I would feel as the tangy treat graced my taste buds with every lick.

One day, I found a German five-mark coin next to the sidewalk. I was deliriously happy. *How many ice cream cones could I buy? Happy! Happy! Joy! Joy!* A never-ending deluge of ice cream for my belly.

The next day, when ice cream music filled the air, I raced as fast as my little legs would carry me. I was the first in line. This was the greatest day of my life. *What good fortune!* I stepped to the window of the ice cream truck and ordered ten lemon ice cream cones.

Oh! All this abundance! My hands were full of ice cream cones. *How in the world will I eat all these ice cream cones before they become a puddle?* A line of ice cream juice ran along the side of one cone. A few drops trickled down my shirt. What was I going to do?

I have a freezer at my house. I could put the ice cream cones in the freezer for later.

I held on tight, switched from a brisk walk to a slight jog, used my elbow to open the apartment building door, and climbed those four flights of stairs. I beamed with delight when I put the ice cream cones in the freezer.

My brother and sister returned from the playground. A huge grin washed over my face as I said, "Look inside the freezer. I got a treat for you!"

Whoever said money can't buy happiness never bought more than one ice cream cone at a time when they were a child.

We work hard for our money, and we need to enjoy the fruits of our labors. When we reward ourselves each quarter with our profit bonus checks, we reinforce profitability. We get a return on the pound of flesh we devote to our business. It is critical for you to give yourself a profit bonus check each quarter. When you do this, you put yourself in alignment with the profit motive that is an integral part of every successful business.

Do not rob yourself by "reinvesting" your reward back into the business. Be a leader and spend this money on yourself so you can experience the joy I did with my lemon ice cream cones. Decades later, it is one of my favorite memories. I still feel the chill of the ice cream on my tongue and smell the citrus as it wafts into my nose.

It doesn't matter how small your profit bonus check is, you can still find something to buy that will give you joy. If all you can afford is a pack of gum, buy your favorite gum and savor each piece more than any gum you've had before. Chew it until all the flavor is gone and your jaw is sore. Your business made a profit. Make it a big deal. Celebrate your profits! You accomplished something momentous. You did it! I'm proud of you!

REACH

The final phase of your Quarterly Celebration is the Reach phase. What do you do when you have a success? Figure out how to repeat it. Success breeds success. Once you experience success, it will be easier to have it again because you've learned what works. Build on the momentum you've created. Establish some objectives for the next three months.

Envision what success will look like for the next three months. What results do you want to obtain? How will you achieve those results? What will you do to increase your profits?

Remember the two sides of the profit coin? You have two types of profitability strategies to consider as you develop your success plan for the next three months: income profitability strategies and expense profitability strategies. Take the time now to write down three income profitability strategies and three expense profitability strategies.

Here are some examples of income profitability strategies:

- Reevaluate your service and/or product pricing
- Generate strategies for expansion and growth
- Evaluate your services and/or products

Here are some examples of expense profitability strategies:

- Cut expenses
- Establish systems and improve their effectiveness, profitability, and efficiency
- Perform an ROI analysis
- Standardize processes
- Delegate lower-level tasks to other employees or vendors

Once you've written down your income and expense profitability strategies, order the items in each category by their level of priority and choose one income profitability strategy and one expense profitability strategy to work on.

Now you have your marching orders for the next three months.

The next step in the Reach phase is to increase your current allocation percentages (CAPs). Compare your CAPs for the last three months with your target allocation percentages (TAPs). Your goal is to increase the CAPs to the **Profit**, **Owner Pay**, and **Tax** accounts by at least 1% each. Remember, you only have one money pie. When you make the profit, owner pay and tax slices larger, the business expense slice must get smaller. Any percentage increase in one area of the money pie will lead to a decrease in another area.

If you still don't receive enough owner pay, then you should prioritize increasing your owner pay percentage until you have enough owner pay each month. If your business does not earn enough to pay you an appropriate amount of money, your business either does not earn enough or it spends too much (or both).

Once your business pays you enough to meet your living expenses, increase your profit percentage. When it comes to permanent profit change in your business, consistent improvement will always lead to more sustainable profit growth than drastic measures.

In the following example, I illustrate how to determine your new CAPs for the next three months. Assume you earn $10,000 per month and your CAPs are at the following percentages:

- Profit 1%
- Owner Pay 40%
- Tax 6%
- Business Expenses 53%

Your goal for the next three months is to increase your profit, owner pay, and tax percentages by 1% each. This means you need to reduce business expenses by 3%.

Let's look at how the math works.

TABLE 27: NEXT QUARTER CAPS			
	Prior Q CAPs	Adjustment	Next Q CAPs
Profit	1%	+1%	2%
Owner Pay	40%	+1%	41%
Tax	6%	+1%	7%
Business Expenses	53%	-3%	50%

You earn $30,000 for the next three months ($10,000/month × 3 months). Each month, You need to reduce business expenses by 3%, or $900, over the next three months. This works out to a $300 reduction in business expenses each month. An extra 1% or $100 will go to each of your **Profit**, **Owner Pay**, and **Tax** bank accounts.

Don't allow yourself to get discouraged by what appears to be a small change right now. We want to make sure this change sticks. Just as big doors swing on little hinges, your big successes are founded on small changes.

You've finished your profitability plan for the next quarter. All you have to do now is stick with it. Grab your calendar and create an appointment three months from now to repeat the Quarterly Celebration process. Continue to do your regular bank transfers. In three months, come back to this chapter. Go through each step of the Quarterly Celebration. You will teach yourself how to grow your profits. Continue with this until you achieve your target profitability.

CHAPTER 10:

THE PROFIT SCOREBOARD

Snot flowed profusely from my nose. The stinging in my eyes was intense. My nose and eyes seemed to compete to see which could produce more liquid. It only took two seconds for the tear gas to humble me.

I was a private in the army, and we were learning how to use our gas masks during Basic Combat Training. Graduation was only a few weeks away.

For a while, my drill sergeants hadn't seemed as intimidating as they did on the first day, when they yelled at all of us to get off the bus and start doing push-ups. But there, in the 100-square-foot-room the army used for NBC (Nuclear, Biological & Chemical) Warfare Training, it was crystal clear to me that the drill sergeants were still in control. I coughed as the noxious fumes permeated my lungs. *Just stay calm. It will be over soon. Once I get out of here, I'll be able to breathe freely again.* I had been ordered to hold both of my arms up level with my shoulders. My right hand kept a tight grip on the gas mask which, a few moments ago, had kept me in fresh air. I was only in that room for a minute or two, but it seemed like five hours.

"Open your eyes, Private!"

Everything in me pushed to keep my eyes shut. However, I knew that once the sergeant saw the whites of my eyes, I would be free from this torture.

"Get outside, Private!"

Relief.

Tears and snot continued to flow. I coughed some more. It was my body's natural way to rid my system of the tear gas. About ten minutes later, the stinging and coughing were done and I began to feel normal again. I could see clearly.

Those minutes in the NBC room were the closest I ever came to losing my sight. My vision helps me process information from the world around me and make decisions. During that training exercise, I suddenly became aware of how much my life would change without it.

Many real estate agents don't yet see clearly when it comes to their money; it's such a confusing subject. Often, agents start their careers fairly ignorant of their business finances.

"Ignorant" may seem harsh because of the contexts in which people tend to use it, which is typically meant as an insult. However, when you look at the definition of "ignorant," you'll realize it is not an unkind word. The *Merriam-Webster Dictionary* defines it as lacking knowledge or comprehension of the thing specified.[24] Ignorance simply means we don't know or understand. How bad is that? Not that bad. Our brains do this fabulous thing called learning. Learning is one of our greatest capacities.

B.B. King, King of the Blues, said, "The beautiful thing about learning is that nobody can take it away from you."[25]

---

[24] Definition of "ignorant," Merriam-Webster.com, accessed October 17, 2021, https://www.merriam-webster.com/dictionary/ignorant.

[25] B.B. King quote. Richard Newman and Julian Bond, *African American Quotations* (Westport, CT: Oryx Press, 1998).

Once you learn how to be financially literate, nobody can take that away from you. It's kind of like riding a bike. Once you learn how to do it, you can't unlearn how to do it. At least that's what I tell myself when I hop on for my annual bike ride.

If you want to be a successful businessperson, you must become financially literate. If you are literate, you know how to read. If you are financially literate, you know how to read your money. How did your world change when you learned how to read words? When you learn how to read your numbers, you'll have the power to transform your business. Understanding your numbers gives you a kind of crystal ball. You'll be able to decipher what works, what doesn't work, and what is likely to work in the future. It's practically impossible to succeed in business without understanding how money works.

I helped Ricardo set up Profit First for Real Estate Agents in his business. During one of our meetings, I asked how things had changed for him in the four weeks we'd been working together.

"Ricardo, before we started working together, what was your view of money?"

"I didn't understand it, it was so complicated. I was confused."

"What about now?"

"It's much easier. Before, I didn't have a system. Now I see more money in my bank account. It's interesting, because now I'm more confident as a businessperson. Before, I would coach my agents, but there was a gnawing pain in my stomach. I looked at my empty bank account and felt like a hypocrite. I thought, *If I'm so successful, why don't I have any money?* Now that I have money, I feel more confident."

When you understand your money, you will make better business decisions. Financial literacy is a critical business skill.

You cannot outsource it. You can hire someone to prepare your financial statements, do your accounting, and keep your books in shape, but if you don't understand what all the financial information means, you are in for a world of hurt. To make matters worse, the bigger your business grows, the more critical financial literacy becomes.

You may have heard someone tell you that you need to understand your P&L statement. What is a P&L statement? How do you get this "key to financial wisdom?" How often should you look at the P&L statement? Did you know there is also a balance sheet and a cash flow statement? Are these important also? Collectively, these documents are called financial statements, and each document has a purpose. The problem many run into is that the accounting rules are inordinately complex. It took me four years of college and multiple years of working as an accountant before I understood how any of it worked.

Many real estate agents look at their financial statements once a month. Some never look at them. The only time they examine their finances is when they give a shoebox full of receipts to their accountants to prepare the tax returns.

Let's remind ourselves why we are in business. We are in business to make money. If we don't manage it, we waste our time, energy and resources. Does it make sense to toil to make our fortunes day after day and then place our cash in a bucket full of big holes? Of course not. When we store our life's work in a hole-ridden pail, we throw a portion of our life away.

If you manage it, your business will run better and get better results. If you don't manage it, your business will struggle.

FINANCIAL STATEMENTS ARE USELESS

Over the past twelve years, I've prepared thousands of financial statements for my clients. About three years ago, I commented to a colleague, "Financial statements are useless. Nobody uses them. What's the point of doing this work few people use?"

For the average person, these are confusing documents. There are two main financial statements: the balance sheet and the income statement (more commonly known as the P&L statement).

The purpose of the balance sheet is to display a business's assets, liabilities, and equity. Assets are what the business owns. Examples of assets are cash, accounts receivable, inventory, vehicles, equipment, intellectual property, computers, and buildings. Liabilities are what the business owes. Examples of liabilities are credit cards, accounts payable, and loans. Equity is what the business is worth. Examples of equity are common stock, owner distributions and draws, and retained earnings.

The balance sheet is divided into two sections: the assets section and the liabilities and equity section. The balance sheet is for a specific day, like the last day of the year, month, etc. If you want to know what your assets and liabilities were at the end of the year, your balance sheet would show total assets, liabilities, and equity for December 31st of that year.

Accountants tell this silly joke:

Why do they call it a balance sheet? Because it balances.

Please don't throw tomatoes at me. I know it's a lousy joke. Maybe this is why many people think accountants are nerdy. Some accountants are funny… which may be another sad attempt at telling you a joke. I'll stop now, before I dig myself too big a hole.

Despite my attempts to be funny, the statement that a balance sheet balances is 100% correct.

Here is the formula for the balance sheet:

ASSETS = LIABILITIES + EQUITY

You can rearrange the formula to determine your company's net worth:

ASSETS − LIABILITIES = EQUITY

That makes sense, right? When we subtract liabilities from assets, we know what we have left over. In other words, we know what the company is worth.

Here's how I explain to my clients what the balance sheet tells us:

OWN − OWE = WORTH

If your business owns more than it owes, then it has a positive worth. For example, if your business has $1,000 in cash and a credit card balance of $400, it is worth $600:

$1,000 − $400 = $600

If your business owns less than it owes, then it has a negative worth. For example, if your business has $500 in cash and a credit card balance of $800, it is worth −$300:

$500 − $800 = −$300

That's pretty much all you need to know about a balance sheet. There are three categories on the balance sheet: assets, liabilities, and equity. The purpose of the balance sheet is to tell you how much you have of each.

The purpose of the income statement is to inform you of how much profit your business does or does not make. It covers a certain a period of time (day, week, month, quarter, year, etc.). It also goes by a few different names, which may be part of the reason why people are confused by it. It is most commonly known as the P&L (profit and loss) statement, however. Let's break down those words:

Profit and loss statement.

Profit is what you have when your business earns more money than it spends. Profit is a good thing in business.

Loss is what you have when your business spends more money than it earns. Loss is a bad thing in business.

The two main sections of the income statement are income and expenses. In the income section, we list our different income sources. In the expenses section, we list all of our expenses.

At the end of a period, we tally up all of our income and all of our expenses. To calculate our profit or lack of profit (a.k.a. loss), we subtract our total expenses from our total income. We either get a profit, signified by a positive number, or a loss, signified by a negative number. Profit and loss are two different results. Either you have a profit, or you have a loss. You don't have both at the same time.

While the income statement can be a useful document, it is incomplete. What you need most is a document that shows you how much money you bring into your business and how much money leaves your business. Two important pieces of data the income statement does not include are how much you pay yourself and how much you pay in taxes. Assuming you have a successful business, both these numbers should be significant. You want to know if your business makes money. In other words, does it create excess cash? The P&L statement does not give you this information.

Many real estate agents are bewildered about financial statements due to the complexity of the rules of accounting.

Some expenditures of money are not expenses. When you purchase a major piece of equipment like a car, it is not an expense, it is a purchase of a fixed asset. When you give the business owner an owner draw or distribution, it is not an expense, it is a reduction of equity, a.k.a. business worth. Are you confused yet? Wait, I'm just getting started. When you make a payment on a loan, only the interest portion of the payment is an expense. The principal payment of the loan is a reduction of the loan, which is either a short-term liability (a liability that will be paid off in less than twelve months) or a long-term liability (a liability that will be paid off in more than twelve months).

There is another document called the cash flow statement. It "explains" the total receipts of cash and total expenditures of cash to business owners. I use the verb "explain" with a grain of salt, because most people with a working brain will never comprehend a cash flow statement. Many CPAs and accountants are just as clueless about it. If your accounting software will prepare a cash flow statement for you automatically, it will be incorrect. To properly prepare one, you need to understand accounting principles. If you don't understand a balance sheet and an income statement, you have a snowball's chance in hell of understanding a cash flow statement.

I only bring up the cash flow statement because it is often the accountant's "solution" for explaining to business owners where all the money comes from and where it goes. While it does technically explain it, it doesn't do so in a way a normal person can understand. I won't spend any more time on it because most people won't be able to read it, let alone understand it. You've now read more about financial statements than most people will ever read in their lives.

There is nothing wrong with you if you are confused by any of these financial statements. You are not the problem. The problem is the financial statements. They were not designed to benefit you. There should be a disclaimer on every financial statement that states:

> **"These financial statements are not**
> **designed for people who don't know how**
> **to read financial statements."**

If you don't understand them, that means you are a smart individual who never suffered a blow to the head with an accounting textbook.

THE PROFIT SCOREBOARD

In traditional accounting, you need to look at all three financial documents to get a complete picture of your business. Then you have to cherry-pick information from each document to garner the information you need to make solid business decisions. Most business owners are already strapped for time and mindshare. You don't need to conform to financial statements that will never serve you. The financial statements need to conform to you. What you need is a simple way to understand your finances—a way that makes sense to you.

I'm mad as hell and I'm not going to take it anymore. It frustrates me that people give their lives to build successful businesses. Business owners are problem-solvers. They improve their communities. They are providers. They are the economic engines of their communities. Yet too many of them fail because they use a systemically broken financial model. Traditional accounting is one of the biggest reasons why people are challenged by the financial side of their businesses. It is not intuitive. It is too convoluted to be of any use to them. I'm sick and tired of it, so I'm doing something now to change the way we understand and use our financial data.

The current system for creating "accurate" financial documents is not designed for business owners. It's designed for investors in publicly traded companies. The rules and regulations in the generally accepted accounting principles (GAAP) are a gargantuan mess too complicated for most people. Many of the regulations and principles in traditional accounting are set up to protect the public from misinterpreting financial data from companies they might buy stock in.

Real estate agents are saddled with an overly complex financial reporting system that isn't suited to their needs. It's also too expensive to administer and manage. Most agents I talk to complain to me about how, every time their previous accountant talked to them, almost everything the bald guy said flew right over their head.

We are not investors in publicly traded companies. We know our businesses inside and out. We don't need the safeguards and regulations traditional accounting dictates to us.

We need a new, single financial document—on one page— that simply explains how a business performs. We need this financial document to be clear, concise, and easy to produce, read and use.

I created a new way for real estate agents to understand their finances. I designed it with you in mind. You want something easy to read that tells you exactly where you stand with your money. I created the Profit Scoreboard to summarize how your business uses money in each of the four key areas of profit, owner pay, tax, and business expenses.

The Profit Scoreboard answers the number one question every real estate agent asks: Do I bring in enough money to pay myself and my expenses? It also factors in the two missing pieces most people don't see when they look at the traditional P&L statement—owner pay and tax.

Here is an example of the Profit Scoreboard:

PROFIT SCOREBOARD

Income	$100,000
Owner's Money	
Owner Pay	35,000
Profit	20,000
Tax	15,000
Total Owner's Money	70,000
Money Available for Business Spending	30,000
Busines Expenses	20,000
Surplus Cash	$10,000

THE THIRD KEY IS YOUR SECURITY SYSTEM

The homes your clients buy with your help will probably be the most expensive things they will ever own. Some of them will chose to protect their homes with an alarm system. It's amazing how security system technology has changed. For a brief period, one of my relatives sold alarm systems. By today's standards, the ones he sold were dinosaurs. They consisted of physical alarms and sensors that attached to doors and windows. Today, you have a smartphone app that will show you who is at your door while your sip your favorite umbrella drink halfway around the world. While the old alarm system works, it is inferior to the advanced security systems you can purchase today.

The Devious Duo existed before you were born and will still be around long after you've graduated from the third rock from the sun. Just because you started using Profit First for your Dream Home Business doesn't mean you are immune to their powers now. You must remain vigilant against these sneaky tree rats.

The Profit Scoreboard is your security system to warn you when The Devious Duo attempt to invade your Dream Home Business. It will help you ignore Bonnie when she shouts, "Sell one more home!" or "Grow, grow, grow!" (Remember, growth for growth's sake doesn't serve you. It must be aligned with what is important to you.) It will also help you shut your ears to Clyde as he beats his constant "Spend everything you make!" refrain.

With our Profit Scoreboard, we get the most vital info we need to manage our finances. Remember, the two golden keys to success with money are:

- **Pay yourself first.**
- **Spend less than you earn.**

The third golden key is observation. Without observation, you won't even know when you pay yourself first or if you spend less than you earn. When you observe, you learn where to improve the return on your investments. You educate yourself by looking at what didn't work out as you planned and why.

You now know the three golden keys of money:

- **Pay yourself first.**
- **Spend less than you earn.**
- **Observe.**

With Profit First, you've learned how to simplify the way you use the money in your business. The Profit Scoreboard simplifies the way you view your money.

CHAPTER 11:

ADVANCED PROFIT FIRST

It was a Monday afternoon. I opened an email from my boss. It read: "Damon, please come to my office."

Great, I thought with dismay. The writing was on the wall.

I put on my game face. As I walked down the hallway to my boss's office, time slowed down. Everything went silent. I walked through his door. His corner office had floor-to-ceiling windows. His mahogany desk was carved with flowers. Behind his chair was a computer table with two monitors and a keyboard. The back of his head showed a bald spot. His fingers danced on the keyboard.

"Have a seat."

I looked at my watch as he typed. Then again. I gulped.

He twirled the chair around.

"Damon, your services are no longer needed. Goodbye."

"Okay," I muttered, and walked out of his office.

I returned to my tiny cubicle. It took me two trips to my car to ferry out all of my belongings. I gave my key to the receptionist as I left for the final time. My face was blank.

On the one hand, I was embarrassed; on the other hand, relieved. I'd thought I was a good employee. I'd always been successful in life. In my hand, the pink slip signified a different message. My confidence was shaken. I was at the bottom of the barrel. I was burned out. I had no idea what to do. *I'll be fine. I've got some savings.*

I thought I had enough money to weather my financial crisis, but a year later, I was still unemployed and the economy was in the dump of the Great Recession. My credit card debt mounted, and my savings shrank with each passing day.

A few months after my termination, I started an accounting business. Over the months, one by one, people hired me. It took me a lot longer than I wanted it to, but I held fast and, little by little, I pulled myself up by the bootstraps.

As I surveyed the ruins of my financial life, I put a simple, three-stage plan in place to get my feet back under me.

STAGE ONE: KEEP THE PERSONAL LIGHTS ON

The first stage is to keep the personal lights on. Until we are fed, with a roof over our head and a shirt on our back, we live in dire poverty. We deserve better. The primary objective is to remove ourselves from personal poverty. In Profit First, we graduate from stage one once we consistently pay ourselves a fair salary: When you look at your Profit Scoreboard, the amount in your owner pay will be enough to cover your living expenses.

STAGE TWO: KEEP THE BUSINESS LIGHTS ON

The break-even point is a momentous occasion, the moment when the business no longer bleeds money. It doesn't come to us begging for another loan, like a snot-nosed, needy cousin with hands outstretched. Along with paying the owner, all the business bills are paid. Everybody is happy. We're ready to move on to stage three.

STAGE THREE: PROFITABILITY

Stage three is when all the blood, sweat, tears, angst, anxiety, and hard work finally bear fruit. Your profits may be small in the beginning, but don't despair. One dollar of profit is worth significantly more than one dollar of loss. One dollar is black and the other is red. With a dollar of profit, you have a viable business. With a dollar of loss, you are doomed to failure until you turn the red ink black.

The goal of every business should be profitability. It's much more important to be profitable than it is to be big. Don't fall into the trap of growth for growth's sake. It only makes sense to grow if you grow profitably. I've written it before, and I'll write it again—here are the two keys to business profitability:

- **Pay yourself first.**
- **Spend less than you earn.**

Paying yourself first means you save money. When you pay yourself first, you create a cash cushion for yourself. Saving is the primary way people become financially free in America. If you do not save money, you will never become wealthy.

In the profitability stage, your business earns more money than it spends. When you look at your bank statement, you see more money at the end of the month than at the beginning. You create surplus cash each month. Extra moolah means you have a business that works. You might say you have a legal money-printing press.

OBLITERATE YOUR DEBT

Many get into debt from time to time. Debt shows up as unpaid accounts payable, unpaid payroll taxes, unpaid credit cards, lines of credit, and loans. When people have debt, it means one thing: they spent money they did not have. Debt places a millstone around your business's neck and shackles around your future success.

Debt may be useful when used to purchase investments. An investment generates more money than it costs and increases the value and earnings potential of your business. Good uses of debt include purchasing assets with a multiple-year life. Another good use of debt is to preserve cash reserves.

A vehicle has a life of at least five years. Say you purchase a $30,000 vehicle and plan to use it for five years. The annual cost to purchase the vehicle is $6,000 ($30,000 ÷ 5 years = $6,000 per year). If you use your $30,000 in cash now to purchase the vehicle, you will be debt-free and own a car free and clear. However, you will have depleted your cash.

Avoid an empty bank account. Cash is the food you feed your business. It may make sense to buy the car with a loan because it will last for many years and keep you flush with moolah. You'll pay rent (otherwise known as interest) in exchange for the ability to pay for the car over time. This is no different than your product—homes. Very few people come to you with an all-cash offer.

People flounder when they have too much debt for their income. How many of your clients had to go with a starter home because their debt-to-income ratio was too high? Some debt is judicious. Too much debt is disastrous.

Strive to remove bad debt from your business. The bad debt people most commonly incur is credit card debt. Annual interest rates are usually north of 18%. Credit card debt is one of the worst profitability vacuums. First, eliminate credit card debt from your business.

You can only extinguish debt with profits from your business. When a business spends more than it earns, it accumulates debt.

When it spends less than it earns, you have surplus cash. You have enough to pay the bills. The first step toward paying off debt is to increase profits. Make more money than you spend. This is the only way you will have money to obliterate the soul-sucking demon of debt.

Here is where the power of habits destroys us. We pay our bills with debt. It is painless in the moment. However, the piper will come to collect on his debts one day. (The piper is always a man. His name is Mr. Meanie Pants.) You may or may not have the cash to pay those bills. You may come face to face with the folly of your ways as you remember how you once proclaimed, "I'll just charge it!"

Some people ignore their debt. They think that if they earn more income, it will somehow solve their problems. As soon as the new money comes in, they've already spent it because it's more fun to buy new things than pay off the debt. Does this sound familiar?

If you ignore debt, it will take over your finances like weeds take over your prize petunias. Debt is a sign of poor health in a business. In other words, debt is a disease. When you have a disease, you need a framework to remove the disease and become healthy again. Until you have a plan to rid yourself of the debt disease, your business will only get sicker.

The first step toward paying off debt is to acknowledge your debt. List all your debts and become aware of the total amount of your debt. You have to live in reality. Until you face your reality, you will be delusional. You can't cure a problem until you have a full picture of it. Until you come face to face with the extent of your debt problem, you will not be able to solve it. Debt problems are not pretty. They are scary. For many people, this is a painful process. You may feel shame as you look at the debt. You may start to belittle yourself because you have debt.

It's normal to feel rotten, but the feeling doesn't need to be permanent. The sooner you deal with your debt, the sooner you move past it.

The second step toward paying off your debt is to live in the pain of the debt. Too much debt puts you at serious risk. It's not bad to suffer. You lived beyond your means, which is unhealthy. How bloated will you be after your Thanksgiving turkey, mashed potatoes, cranberry sauce, sweet potatoes with those devilish marshmallows, and pumpkin pie? You ate too much. Too much food in your precious belly isn't conducive to your good health. If you are ashamed about your debt, lean into the shame. Use it as a tool to crush your debt.

Now is the time to change your future. Change your present. Kapow your debt with a profitable business. You only pay off debt with profits. Otherwise, you will continue to rob Peter to pay Paul and eventually Peter will be dead. Who will you rob then?

In step three, you implement the debt freeze. The law of holes states: If you find yourself in a hole, stop digging. Do not incur any additional debt. Stop digging. If you use a credit card, don't use it anymore. Use a debit card instead. I don't care if you get airline miles or cash back rewards. Those "rewards" are what got you into this mess.

When you pay a bill with your credit card and carry a credit card balance, you choose to spend either past or future earnings. When you spend past earnings, you deplete your savings. When you spend future earnings, you bet you will make enough money to pay the debt and live your life. It's easy to be overly optimistic about tomorrow when the sun shines brightly today. What if a tornado runs through your neighborhood tomorrow? You'll need to hire someone to remove the tree that laid its head, ever so gently, on your garage. Murphy's Law will jump up from behind the bushes and laugh at you. Ha, ha, ha. Decide, today, to be profitable. This means that from now on, you will only spend money you have in the present.

The only way you will ever pay off your debts is with profit from your business. When you have cash after you pay all your bills, you have profit.

Debt is not evil. Yes, you should pay off debt and reduce unnecessary expenses so you are not weighed down by unmanageable debt. However, money in the bank provides a cash cushion for the day when Murphy throws a curveball. When you save money, you prevent future debt. Save money while you pay off debt.

When you earn extra money in your business, split those funds between savings and debt reduction. The simple formula I use when I have extra money is, half of it goes to savings and half pays down debt.

Reinforce the correct behaviors. When you save money, you get the positive reward of more money in the bank. Money in the bank account is more beautiful than a calico cat giving a beagle a back massage. When you pay down debt, you remove the consequences of bad money habits.

If you take the alternative approach and devote all your profit to lowering debt, you will have a lower debt balance. But you won't have any money in the bank. While it's good to pay down debts, it isn't as rewarding as cash in the bank. I love it when my bank account grows. Continually reinforce the right money habits. The first money habit you must have in place is saving money. Never stop saving money. If all you can save is one dollar, save one dollar. Everyone can afford to save one dollar.

Don't underestimate the power of small actions. The direction you are headed in is more important than the speed at which you travel. When you take the right actions, you will get the right results.

COMBATING SEASONALITY

The natural business cycle of real estate leads many to a feast-or-famine cycle. The time to make hay in the real estate industry usually occurs during the spring and summer months. Every summer, you may forget how painful the slow times were as you back truckloads of cash into your bank account. Most real estate agents spend everything they make. They live high off the hog during the spring and summer. Once the winter sets in, dry dog chow becomes the food du jour. A lot of meals are in a $15.99, thirty-five-pound bag of Lassie's Delight.

To avoid the pain of the slow months, stop chasing squirrels and start acting like squirrels. Squirrels collect nuts every year. As soon as it becomes warm enough to collect nuts and other food, squirrels gather and store food for the next winter. Winter will return, and they prepare for when the food is gone. They store their treasures in a squirrel vault that holds all the collected food so they have enough to last through the winter months. You would be wise to follow the squirrel's instinctual behavior. The squirrel wakes up each morning and collects and carries food off to her vault. Does the squirrel say, "What should

TABLE 28: SEASONALITY					
	Jan	Feb	Mar	Apr	May
Deposits					
Spending					
Money Kept					

I do today?" No, she just works. No thinking needed. Just work. On to the most important task. If Harriet the squirrel doesn't do her job, she will starve in a few months.

The preparation phase is a continual process. It's time to squirrel up some money so you'll be prepared when you enter the slower months of the year. Use a **Vault** account to save cash throughout the year. Then, when you have slower months, you will have enough to weather the winter. I'll explain more about the **Vault** account a little later in this chapter.

Use the Seasonality table to prepare for your next winter. Create your own version of Table 28 on a piece of paper.

Write down your total deposits from each month's bank statements. Next, write down your total spending from each month's bank statements. For each month, subtract the spending from your deposits and enter the amount in the Money Kept row for that month. For example, in January, you deposited $7,000 into your bank account. You spent $7,500. Your money kept amount for January is −$500. Fill out the entire table.

Highlight the three months with the least amount of money kept. Add those three numbers together to determine how much money you need in savings to prepare for next year's low months. If you have more than three months with negative numbers, you should highlight those numbers as well.

SEASONALITY, continued						
Jun	Jul	Aug	Sep	Oct	Nov	Dec

For example, let's assume that when we add up all our negative months for the prior twelve months, we had a total cash shortfall of $25,000. If we don't change anything, we will find ourselves in the same position next year. We should deposit at least $25,000 into our savings account during the next twelve months to prepare for the winter months, when things get tight.

How much better will you feel when you have enough cash to weather the winter months of your business? Find a pen and a piece of paper and write down what it will be like when you don't have to worry about money during the next twelve months. Envision how a profitable business will change your life.

What happens if you have zero negative cash months during the next twelve months? You have extra money. What emotions do you feel now?

You just spent some time in the future, where you have a business free of financial worries because you set aside at least $25,000 for your low months and you rest easier at night. Come back to today. Do you want to create your new future? If the answer is yes, prepare now and set aside enough cash so your business will weather the storms life throws at you.

If your business generates more money than it is spends, you should have zero months with a negative number. If you have a few months with negative amounts in the Money Kept row, you will experience a cash crunch in the next twelve months. History tends to repeat itself. Prepare for this lack of money. Lower your expenses to match your revenue. Set money aside now for cash shortfall months.

Many people revert to credit cards when they have cash shortfalls. This is a disastrous strategy because of the exorbitant interest rates credit card companies charge. While the extra interest is bad, what is worse for people is spending more than they make. Consequently, they lose touch with the reality of how much it costs to run their business. If you pay a low interest rate—below 5%, for example—you still spend more money than you make. Don't spend more than you make. You have two fundamental money principles. Disregard these money principles at your peril. Remember the three golden keys of money:

- **Pay yourself first.**
- **Spend less than you earn.**
- **Observe.**

We tend to revert to our historical behaviors. Unless we consciously change our present, we will do the same things over and over again because they are in our comfort zones. We enjoy our comfort zones. They are aptly named because they are comfortable. However, our comfort zones keep us entrenched in old behaviors, actions, and results. They limit our growth at best and destroy us at worst.

In November, 2019, I took Chris through my Six Steps to Profit First Success Program. I called him a year later to see how he was doing. He was so excited to give me his update.

"Damon, I have $85,000 more in my bank account than I had a year ago."

"$85,000! Are you serious?"

"Yes."

"How much of it would you attribute to the work you and I did together last year?"

"All of it."

"Wow, I'm so happy for you."

To put this in context, four months after I helped Chris set up Profit First in his business, COVID-19 killed hundreds of thousands and shuttered many businesses. Chris followed Profit First and thrived despite a challenging economy.

VAULT ACCOUNT

On August 27, 2006, Comair Flight 5191 scooted along the runway at around 6:07 EDT at the Blue Grass Airport in Fayette County, Kentucky. Comair Flight 5191 was assigned to use runway 22 for the takeoff. However, the pilot made a fatal mistake and used runway 26.

Runway 22 is 7,003 feet long.

Runway 26 is 3,503 feet long.

Fifty people boarded the airplane.

Moments after the plane throttled its engines, forty-nine people perished as the plane crashed.

Choose the right runway. It was a matter of life and death for the pilot, crew, and passengers of an airplane.

Every flight begins when a plane departs the airport terminal and rolls toward the runway. Engines go to full thrust. The plane launches into the air. What happens if the runway ends before the plane gathers enough speed to take flight? The case of Comair Flight 5191 makes the results all too clear.

Money in the bank is your runway. More money equals a longer runway. You want a long enough runway for the airplane of your business to take flight.

When the runway is too short, problems occur. Let's go further and translate the money runway into months of cash.

The **Vault** account is one of my favorite bank accounts. Its primary purpose is to store money. Do you remember the last time you went to the bank? At my bank, the vault has a three-foot-thick, round metal door with a big metal wheel that looks like a ship's helm. You turn the wheel, push down a handle, and pull open the massive door.

The **Vault** account protects your money. It is where you build and store your cash reserves.

How much money does your business spend in a month? If it spends $10,000, you need $10,000 in cash to have a one-month runway.

3 months = $30,000
6 months = $60,000
12 months = $120,000

If you have one month's worth of runway cash, you won't live paycheck to paycheck. If you have three months' worth, you won't have to worry about annual seasonality. If you have six months' worth, you'll be able to weather a downward shift in the economy. If you have twelve months' worth of cash, you'll survive a major recession or depression. I can't describe the relief I feel because I have a long enough cash runway.

Let's look at a successful company. Apple Inc. generated $265 billion in sales for the year ending September 29, 2018. It had $25 billion in cash, or roughly 9% of revenues. It also had $40 billion in marketable securities. Marketable securities are almost as good as cash. The company's business expenses for the year amounted to $30 billion, and it had almost enough cash on hand to operate for a year with no sales. If you add the marketable securities to cash, it had about two years' worth of runway. Apple Inc. has a lot of stability.

The first cash goal of every company should be to have a minimum of one month in savings. I've talked with many business owners who say, "I prefer not to see cash in my bank account because I get a better return when I spend it on marketing." I get it. A higher return on investment is important. However, cash in the bank is about stability. First, a business must have stability. Otherwise, it will crash and burn.

The **Vault** account is the bank account where you build your cash reserves. I set up this bank account as a savings account. I want to earn a little bit of interest. My money makes little money babies. Oh! I just shed a tear. Rejoice.

The initial percentage I use for this bank account is 1%. When you do your bank transfers, 1% of your net commission income goes to the **Vault** account. Leave the CAPs at 1% until your business operates at its TAPs. When money gets tight, go to your **Vault** account to cover the lean months.

COST OF SALES AND NET COMMISSION INCOME ACCOUNTS

The **Cost of Sales** bank account is for when you pay commissions directly to your team of agents. Many national real estate companies provide back-office services, such as issuing commission split payments to your agents. They also issue everyone their 1099s at the end of each year. If a back office pays your agents and you don't issue commission splits, you can skip this section.

If you own a private real estate agency and you pay your team of agents, you will set up the following two checking accounts:

- **Cost of Sales**, to issue commission split payments to your team and referral partners
- **Net Commission Income**, where you transfer your portion of the commission

Here's how the money flows through your bank accounts:

1. First, deposit your gross commission income into your **Income** account.
2. Transfer the commission split for your agents to the **Cost of Sales** bank account.

3. Transfer the remaining portion to the **Net Commission Income** bank account.

A typical commission would work like this. Assume a buyer's agent gets 40% of the gross commission income. In this example, the gross commission income for a transaction is $10,000. $4,000 goes to the buyer's agent and $6,000 goes to your company.

The $10,000 is deposited into the **Income** account. Transfer $4,000 to the **Cost of Sales** bank account and $6,000 to the **Net Commission Income** bank account. Pay $4,000 to the buyer's agent. When you get to your bank transfer days, you will transfer money out of your **Net Commission Income** account, based on your current allocation percentages, to the **Profit**, **Owner Pay**, **Tax**, and **Business Expenses** bank accounts.

RESEARCH AND DEVELOPMENT (R&D) ACCOUNT

The **Research and Development (R&D)** account is the permission account for you to try new things with your business. I'd love for you to never chase squirrels again, but I recognize that trying to convince you not to is a fool's errand. Besides, squirrel-chasing can be fun. Will Bonnie sing a new song today? Will Alvin (wait, he was a chipmunk, ugh) show you his latest tap dance routine? What new post-impressionist masterpiece will Josephine paint with her brush made of silvertip badger hair? Just don't chase five hundred gold-sequined jacket-wearing squirrels. Instead, limit how many squirrels you chase.

The **R&D** account puts boundaries around how many squirrels you chase. With the money in this account, you experiment to determine where you can get a better return.

Each month, this account will get some money as part of your regular bank transfers. Maybe it is a percentage of net commission income or a set dollar amount. When you want to try a new marketing method, use money from this account. Now you have some funds to test. You limit your risk because you limit how much is available to spend on untested initiatives.

MONTHLY BUSINESS EXPENSES TRANSFER

Once you've established the right systems in your business, you may find that your business expenses are the same each month. You review your records and determine that you spend an average of $10,000 per month. You've established a rhythm. When you do your bank transfers, transfer your NCI from the **Income** account to each of your **Profit**, **Owner Pay**, **Tax**, and **Business Expenses** accounts.

When you sell more houses than usual, you earn more money. In those months, you'll transfer more money into your **Business Expenses** account than you usually need. Let's say that last month, because you had more transactions than you normally do, you transferred $19,000 into your **Business Expenses** account.

You may have heard of Parkinson's Law, where our demand is directly tied to the resources available to us? We now have an extra $19,000 available to spend in our **Business Expenses** account. According to Parkinson's Law, we will spend the extra cash without thinking about it. It's as if Clyde, The Human Problem, comes to us with a red bandana around his face and yells at us to put our hands up as he pilfers the money from our pockets.

Meanwhile, Bonnie sings a beautiful song to appease the pain we experience when we shake out our empty wallets. She's such a siren. Nobody can resist her angelic voice—especially when she sings "London Bridge Is Falling Down." Then she winks. My heart swoons.

When your bank transfers provide you with more money in your **Business Expenses** account than you need to spend, it is easy to spend that extra because it's in the bank. You may be tempted to crawl back to the life where you threw money into a bonfire, only to receive smoke and ash.

There are two ways to preserve your funds when you have excess money in your **Business Expenses** account:

- Lower your business expenses percentage
- Create a monthly limit for how much you put into the **Business Expenses** account

When you lower your business expenses percentage, you increase the percentage allocation to your **Profit**, **Owner Pay**, and/or **Tax** accounts.

With a monthly business expenses limit, you determine a maximum amount that will go into the **Business Expenses** account each month. For example, you may set a monthly limit of $10,000. Once you've deposited $10,000 into the **Business Expenses** account, transfer the remaining amount to your **Vault** account. In our example above, we had $19,000 allocated to our business expenses. We would transfer $10,000 to the **Business Expenses** account and then transfer $9,000 to the **Vault** account.

The added side benefit of this is, you build your cash reserves. You started your savings with one single, singing dollar. How amazing would it be to have a choir the size of

Alaska, accompanied by a full orchestra as they sing and play the "Hallelujah Chorus"? It's a joy to have a ton of scratch in your bank account. Cash reserves stabilize your business. As you build your cash reserves, you gain more power, calm, clarity, and confidence in your business. Cash is king!

CHAPTER 12:

THE WORLD IS YOUR OYSTER

One afternoon, I hung up my car keys and heard the pitter patter of feet grow louder as they pounded the hardwood floor.

"Daddy!"

I squatted, extended my arms and caught my son Levi. I held him to my heart so tightly. *Don't let go until he lets go. You only have a season to enjoy this.*

"Daddy, I want to learn how to swim."

"Okay, let's eat dinner, and we'll go to the pool."

We got our swimsuits and towels and drove two miles to the swimming pool. I'm an average swimmer at best. I know how to do the breaststroke, the sidestroke, and the American crawl. I learned them all for my Boy Scout swimming merit badge.

We took our pre-swim shower and dipped our toes into the water. Why does the water always feel like ice at first, no matter how warm it is? *I just need to bite the bullet and jump in.* I pinched my nose, closed my eyes and—splash! After a few seconds in the water, my body adjusted to the temperature and I was as happy as a pig in mud.

Levi, who was five at the time, waddled into the water. *I've never taught anyone to swim. How will I teach my boy to swim?* I remembered the lessons I'd received. *I'll just teach Levi what my swimming teachers taught me.*

As I pondered Levi's request, I decided to start at the beginning. At least 75% of swimming is floating. Once a person learns how to float, they can move across the surface of the water. Without the ability to float, they will sink to the bottom like a rock. This is not the result I wanted for my only son. I need him to carry on the family name.

I'll teach Levi how to float. To float, one must relax. Many people freak out when they first enter the water. Splish splash, they are not taking a bath. They wail, scream, and flail their arms and legs. This is the worst thing they can do. They cannot relax while they freak out. They must act against their instincts of terror. They must be calm. My entire goal was to calm Levi so he could control his body. *Once he relaxes, he'll float.*

"Lie on your back, Levi, I'll hold you above the water with my hands." I placed both of my hands under Levi's back to give him some support as he began his lesson.

"Good. Now reeeeelaaaaaax."

I removed my hands. He sank like his trunks were made of cement, swallowed some water and began to cough. We tried again. I placed my hands under Levi's back until he was able to float, then removed my hands. He stayed afloat for two seconds. Then four seconds.

Now he's got it. I beamed. "I'm so proud of you Levi!" We continued our game to see how long he could float. By the end of our swimming lesson, he had floated for sixty-five seconds straight. I was thrilled for him. I felt honored. He had enough faith in me to listen as I taught him how to float. It was a huge accomplishment for Levi. I smile as I think about our swimming lesson.

A few days later, basking in joy as I thought about how my boy learned how to float, I recognized that there was something for me to learn from his swimming lesson. If you want to swim, the first thing to master is floating. Without the ability to float, one cannot swim. People waste a ton of energy as they flail their arms and kick their feet to no avail. If they do this too much, they are destined to sink to a watery grave. You must learn how to float. Floating is the key to life when you choose to enter the water.

In business, profitability is akin to floating. The first thing to master is profitability. Without profit, your business will run out of money. Your business will sink and drown you in the process since we, as ordinary citizens, are not allowed to print money. (It's a federal crime. The government is the only entity with the legal power to print money.)

You have profit when your business earns more money than it spends. There are two sides to the profit coin: earn more and spend less.

Profit is the most important business measurement. If your business doesn't create profit, you don't have a business, you have an expensive hobby. When you have profit, you will have cash in the bank. If you don't have cash in the bank, it is a clear sign your business is not profitable.

Your business must be profitable.

Most people who enter the real estate world jump in with everything they've got. Very few people who do so have ever run a business before. It takes a lot more than sales and negotiation skills to become a successful real estate agent. More agents would be successful if they acted more like businesspeople.

WHY YOU SHOULD LOVE BUSINESS OWNERSHIP

Twenty-five years ago, I made the fateful decision to start my first business. It forever transformed my life—and it was a complete disaster. I bled money each month and struggled to find new customers. It wasn't a real business. It was an expensive hobby. Finally, I got real with myself and called it quits.

A few years passed, and I saw a new opportunity. While looking at a bulletin board in Nelson Hall at North Carolina State University, I found an advertisement from someone named Suzi Caldwell, announcing the sale of her janitorial business. I was intrigued. I had just finished my army enlistment and returned to college to earn my accounting degree. I wrote down Suzi's contact info and headed into my next class. It was hard for me to concentrate on my professor's words. My mind raced with the idea of Suzi's business.

Things will be different this time. If I bought her business, I would already have a customer base. I wouldn't have to start from scratch; the business already made money. Anticipation ran through my veins. I had a chance to run a real business. Maybe I could shake off the self-doubt and shame from my previous business failure.

After some due diligence, I concluded that buying the business made sense. Over the next few months, Suzi taught me everything about her business. I cleaned toilets. I knocked on doors to get new customers. I took out the garbage. I was happy.

In August, 2000, my new bride Angel and I became the owners of A-1 Cleaning. I learned how to run a business by mopping floors, taking out trash, and vacuuming carpets. I later went to business school and invested tens of thousands of dollars on a graduate degree. As much as I loved my academic experience, I learned more from my years at A-1 Cleaning than I did in the ivory halls of the graduate degree program.

Entrepreneurship is the best career decision I've made in my life. Most of our decisions in life are inconsequential. Only a few dictate the quality of our lives. One of these is the career we choose—one of the most important decisions we make. Many people wish they could be their own boss. Business ownership is not without risk, and it is not for the faint of heart. But it remains the best bastion of opportunity in America. You have unlimited potential. You serve people. You have the best opportunity to gain freedom and control over your life.

The path of business ownership is a path of constant improvement. I've always had to grow as a person before I realized business growth. The person I've become as a result of my business is my greatest reward.

Business ownership is the best way to take hold of your birthright of freedom. Ups and downs will come and go. You'll continually face your fears and figure out new and better ways to conquer those fears. You may suffer humiliating defeats in business. Those defeats will change you. Your business will enable you to grow to a new level.

Your business is a path of unlimited potential. You are on a heroic journey. You'll serve people in exciting new ways. You'll impact your clients. And when you change lives, you change. The best way to live a life of abundance is to grow a successful, profitable business. You are part of an elite group of individuals in the world. Honor your status as a business owner and choose success.

HOW TO DEAL WITH FAILURE

To err is human…

We, as humans, are imperfect. It's easy to be hard on ourselves when we fail. Somehow, we view failure as a bad thing; but if we don't fail, it means we aren't trying hard enough. You cannot achieve success without trying something new. Whenever we try something new, we will stumble and fail until we get better. We cannot circumvent failure on our path to greatness.

I use three tools to overcome failure and help me put it in proper perspective. I don't want negativity to chip away at my self-confidence.

- I reflect on my past failures.
- I do less to do more.
- I take a break.

Why should you reflect on your past failures? This may seem counterproductive or counterintuitive at first. Here's why you should revisit your past failures. Failures are temporary. Also, they are events. Not people.

Here are a few of my failures. I dropped out of college three times. I started college when I was eighteen and graduated when I was twenty-eight. I used to berate myself for my college failures—no longer. It doesn't matter how long it took me to finish my first college degree; I still have a diploma. It took me longer than I intended, but I still finished. I have my college degree. Nobody can take that accomplishment away from me. The three times I dropped out don't matter.

You have your own accomplishments. What failures did you go through to reach your successes? Sometimes we fail because we weren't good enough—yet. We may have needed those failures as wake-up calls. We may have needed those failures to force us to take stock of what we did and change course to become better.

As you change, you improve. Your failures are and will be crucial building blocks of your future success. Failure is not a bad thing. Failure is a stepping-stone to better. While I'm not on a mission to fail, I don't let failure keep me from progress. Failure is an integral part of success. I spent forty-five years feeling scared of failure. I thought I had to be perfect.

It's important to get back in the saddle and try again. However, at some point, you have to look to see if the saddle you sit atop is attached to a stationary sawhorse instead of a living, breathing animal.

For two weeks in Army Basic Combat Training, I learned how to shoot an M16 rifle. It wasn't easy for me. I had a condition called left eye dominance. This would have been fine if I was left-handed. However, I am right-handed. I had to make constant adjustments to compensate for the way I looked through the rifle sight.

I got frustrated when I missed the targets. My drill sergeant, while firm with me, worked to build my confidence. When I failed to hit the paper target, he took me back to the basics and we focused on the four fundamentals of marksmanship: steady position, aim, breath control, and trigger squeeze. My drill sergeant took the time to review each of these four fundamentals with me. As he observed me, he pointed out where I needed to improve. As I mastered each of the fundamentals, I learned how to shoot and hit my target. Eventually, I became a good enough marksman to pass the test.

I still haven't met anyone who gets more than twenty-four hours a day. If everyone has the same amount of time, why do some people get more from their time? Because they invest their time in things that produce better results.

Pause for a moment. Do you hear that?

It's Vilfredo Pareto singing a ditty about the 80/20 rule from his grave.

You will accomplish more if you do less. Additionally, you will enjoy your life more. Assume you work five days a week.

What's 20% of five? One day. Is it possible to get 80% of your results in just one day per week? Yes, if you focus on the most important thing.

Let's take this a step further. Assume you work an eight-hour day. What's 20% of an eight-hour day? About an hour and a half. Is it possible for you to produce 80% of your results for a day in an hour and a half? Yes, if you focus on the most important thing.

When you focus on doing only the most important thing in your business, you reduce your workload down to the best use of your time. Here are three questions to think about:

- If you only had an hour and a half to work this week, what would you do?
- How would your life improve if you did more of the one-and-a-half-hour work?
- What will you stop doing now so you can do more of your one-and-a-half-hour work?

The third way to recover from failure is to take a break. When I commit, I put everything I have into what I've committed to. Sometimes this leads to tunnel vision. While this type of behavior has been critical to my success, it also hinders me at times. Sometimes I tell myself that I just need to try harder, I just need to put more time in. Sometimes the answer is less work. When I develop tunnel vision, I get lost in the weeds. I become so task-oriented, I lose sight of my overarching strategy. It's as if I'm driving toward California at a hundred miles per hour when my desired destination is New York City. It doesn't matter how fast I go if I'm headed in the wrong direction.

When I take a break, it gives me time to separate myself from the here and now and reconnect with the larger strategy.

When I take a break, I give myself time to breathe, remove myself from any ruts I've dug myself into, and get back on the path of success.

Failure can be a source of great pain when we allow it to be; we are always in control of how we react. When we berate ourselves for our failures, we diminish our ability to succeed. When we berate ourselves, we focus on what doesn't work instead of what does. Give yourself some grace. Failure is only temporary. We can always get back in the saddle and reconnect with success. Failure is a stepping-stone to success. We grow as we fail forward.

Next time you fall short, acknowledge it, give yourself some grace, and try again. It doesn't matter how many times you fail as long as you learn from it, improve, and persist.

JUST GET STARTED

My legs throbbed with pain. Tears ran down my cheeks. I walked slowly as I followed a line of people. I felt defeated, though it should have been a joyous event. A young Marine Corps officer placed the marathon finisher medal around my neck. I grinned, bore it, and thanked her.

As I walked to meet my family, my mind went into overdrive. I thought about how the journey began when, a year earlier, I started my training with a two-mile run with my friend Jerry. I then reflected on the last 26.2 miles. *I started off too quickly. My weekly mileage was too high three weeks ago. I should have rested more last week.* My mind continued to list twenty more ways I could have run the race differently.

The next day, I looked at the marathon map and felt awe. I completed 26.2 miles. I did it. I accomplished my goal. I absorbed the moment. Then a thought pierced my mind.

The secret to finishing a marathon is to put one foot in front of the other for 26.2 miles.

I've started many adventures as an ignorant fool:

- I went off to college.
- I got married.
- I started a family.
- I started a business.
- I started another business.
- I started a third business.
- I started a fourth business.
- I flew to Europe.
- I flew to Europe two more times.
- I ran a marathon. Then another six.
- I started a blog.
- I wrote a book. Then two more books.
- I started a podcast.

I had no idea how much work was involved when I embarked on any of these adventures. However, before I took the plunge, I did decide that each of them was a good idea. If I had known the challenges I would go through when I started, it is unlikely I would have begun any of these journeys.

Some of my adventures have been worthwhile. Others have been learning experiences I simply struggled through. I'm grateful that I started each journey as an ignorant fool; the good I've received from each adventure has far outweighed the pain, toil, and heartache. If I had not been ignorant, I would have quit too early. I would never have tasted the fruits of success.

This reminds me of when I've watched each of my four children learn how to walk. They learned to walk by observation. They stood. They fell. They stood and then fell on their bums. Then they fell on their faces. They experienced a lot of failures as toddlers until they learned how to control their bodies enough to perform the intricate dance of one foot in front of the other.

You succeed by consistently and persistently putting one step in front of the other. This takes repetition, and you will have to do it long enough to achieve the desired results. So what? It doesn't matter as long as the objective is important to you. Progress is progress.

The biggest lesson I learned from each of my journeys is the value of persistence. While I'd love to hit a home run, it's unlikely to happen today. Often, what I do is ordinary. Most of it goes unnoticed.

However, daily, persistent actions compound in a remarkable fashion. Consistent, focused action produces tremendous results over time. Calvin Coolidge said, "Nothing in the world can take the place of persistence. Talent will not; nothing is more common than unsuccessful men with talent. Genius will not; unrewarded genius is almost a proverb. Education will not; the world is full of educated derelicts. Persistence and determination alone are omnipotent."[26]

Most of us spend our time on unimportant activities. We binge on television. We enjoy the entertainment, but reap no significant results. Nothing will happen until you take the first step. Once you take the first step, you get what you need to take the second step. One step at a time is all you need. Just get started. The path will reveal itself with every new step.

---

[26] Calvin Coolidge quote from a program at a Coolidge memorial service (1933), cited in *The Oxford Dictionary of Quotations, Fifth Edition*, ed. Elizabeth Knowles and Angela Partington (Oxford, England: Oxford University Press, 1999).

TAKE THE PROFIT FIRST CHALLENGE

Desire profitability more than anything in your business. Vow to pay yourself first. Spend less than you earn. Don't overcomplicate the simplicity of business profitability. Profit is simple. Don't mess it up. When you pay yourself first and spend less than you earn, you give yourself the best chance at profitability.

If you know how to add and subtract, you have all the math skills you will ever need to master business finance. What will you do with the knowledge you've gleaned from this book? Will you act on it to build a permanently profitable real estate business? If you put this book down and let it collect dust, you may as well never have read it.

Until you act on the knowledge I've given you, it will remain useless. Your action applied to the knowledge is the key to more cash in the bank. Action trumps knowledge every time.

One of my clients, Angie, is very successful. She never finished college. She worked for a while in the restaurant industry. She loved interacting with people, so she decided to try her hand as a real estate agent.

She was seven months pregnant when she started her education, and weeks away from single motherhood. After she got her license, she started her career with a builder. After a few years, she didn't make enough, so she moved on to something else.

Then she found a real estate team to work with and something clicked. She started to achieve the success she had dreamt of so many years before, when she was weighed down by her seven-months-pregnant belly.

When Angie hired me, she lived from commission check to commission check. From time to time, she needed to borrow money to make ends meet until she sold a house and got her next commission check. Then she started her brokerage firm and built a team.

In 2018, she sold around 180 homes. I told her about Profit First for Real Estate Agents, and we set it up in her business. Over the next eighteen months, she followed the system and cash grew in her bank accounts.

In 2019, she asked me, "Shouldn't I invest the money in the stock market to get a better return on investment?"

"No," I replied, "your business needs to have liquid cash. We've been on the longest economic expansion in history. A shift will come soon, and the economy will go into a recession. It's the natural business cycle. The economy expands, hits a peak, and then recedes. Once the recession hits bottom, the economy expands again."

Over the next eighteen months, Angie saved about $200,000. Then, in March, 2020, COVID-19 plunged the country into a recession I never thought I would see. Unemployment rose to the double digits, and many lost their lives. I can't begin to tell you how good it felt to know I had counseled Angie to build a war chest of cash that she could use as a buffer during the pandemic.

Angie told me, "Profit First is absolutely amazing! This year, I have netted several hundred thousand more than I did last year. I also eliminated $100,000 in marketing expenses, but our real estate team has sold over a hundred more homes than last year. The system allows you to get control of your finances and truly understand where money is going. It's life-changing."

You owe it to yourself to be successful. If you've been given the vision to start a business and put everything on the line, you've received a gift.

Don't hide your gift. Be a hero to yourself and everyone who knows you. Don't shirk the responsibility you have to be successful. You have a sacred calling. It will improve people's lives.

We live in a fabric of humanity, where our actions matter. When you improve your life, it improves the lives of those connected to you.

We were born into this world to make a difference. Answer the call of greatness.

Choose success.

I'M GLAD I DID...

The late financing pioneer R. Nelson Nash shared a great nugget of wisdom in a podcast I listened to recently. To paraphrase him:

First you prepare the soil. Then you plant the corn. After a while, the corn comes up, and you get something else you didn't plant. Weeds. Now you have a huge crop of weeds that covers up the corn. When you remove the weeds, the corn sticks out like a sore thumb. The problem is excess baggage. Weeds take over and divert you from the original crop. You developed the farm for the corn. Not the weeds.[27]

The weeds always pop up. They are pernicious. We must be vigilant and continually remove them. They suck up our time, money, and—perhaps most importantly—our focus.

Too many agents are distracted by the faulty thinking that they just need to sell one more house to get ahead. When you use Profit First in your business, you remove the weeds that obscure the most important crop of your business—cash. When you have profit, your bank balance increases with every new home

---

[27] R. Nelson Nash interview, "Episode 52: The Case for IBC: Chapter 4, Becoming Your Own Banker," Lara-Murphy Reporting, April 10, 2018. https://lara-murphy.com/podcast/episode-52-the-case-for-ibc-chapter-4-becoming-your-own-banker/, accessed October 18, 2021.

sale. You remove yourself from the hamster wheel of chasing the next home sale as the cure for your business woes.

When you have a working money system, everything else in your business improves. Your confidence improves. Consequently, you sell more homes. You make better decisions. Your business works better. You have the money to enjoy what you value most.

The best thing you can do for your business today is to make it more profitable. Profit First gives you a proven, simple system to ensure that your profits grow, month in and month out. It works regardless of how many homes you sell each year. It works for those who sell less than ten homes per year. It works for those who sell hundreds and even thousands of homes per year. It is built on the three golden keys of money:

- **Pay yourself first.**
- **Spend less than you earn.**
- **Observe.**

When you follow these rules, you guarantee your money success. You transition to a point where money is no longer a limiting factor. When you spend less than you earn, you will not need to worry about running out of money. It is impossible to run out of money when you spend less than you earn.

Profit First is the best money system for real estate agents. It reminds us that the most important component of our business is profit. Profit is simply cash in the bank. If we don't have cash in the bank, we don't have a successful business.

Lewis Hamilton, the champion Formula One race car driver, said, "Everyone has complicated lives, but the more you can simplify it and make it work for you, the better it is going to be."[28]

---

[28] "Lewis Hamilton Quotes," BrainyQuote.com, accessed October 18, 2021, https://www.brainyquote.com/quotes/lewis_hamilton_872408.

Over the next twenty years, millions of dollars will flow in and out of your real estate business. At the end of those twenty years, you will have one of these two thoughts:

- I'm glad I did.
- I wish I had.

Which thought do you want to experience?

ACKNOWLEDGMENTS

My primary goal when I started this book was to write a book that would stand on its own. I didn't want it to be a cookie cutter version of the original *Profit First*. Real estate agents needed a book written to help them seize opportunities and protect them from Bonnie and Clyde, The Devious Duo.

I didn't realize how this book would change me as I went through numerous editing rounds, scrapping what I thought was beautiful a few months earlier in favor of something simpler and more impactful, a better way to explain a point with a new and vibrant story. Most of all, writing this book helped me realize that my purpose is to simplify money.

While I wrote the words, it took a team of devoted professionals to craft my words into this book. I'm thankful my team was full of champions.

Thank you to Anjanette Harper, my editor, whose "Reader First" refrain taught me that this book isn't about me: It's for you, the reader. Anjanette, you helped me craft a book that I will always be proud of.

Thank you, Zoë Bird, my copyeditor, for you attention to detail. It was a delight working with you.

Thank you, Olaf Nelson, my typesetter, for transforming my manuscript into a beautifully designed book.

Thank you, Mike Michalowicz, for your Profit First message. It changed my life for the better. I've been blessed to see many of my clients' lives transformed by the pay-yourself-first method applied to business.

Thank you to all the real estate agents I've met and will continue to meet over my career. You are some of the savviest business owners I know.

Thank you, Angel. I love the life we've built together.

APPENDIX:

CREATE YOUR PROFIT
FIRST TIMELINE

Most people who start Profit First for Real Estate Agents want to improve their profitability. The biggest culprit when it comes to low profits is too much money spent on business expenses. Reduce your business expenses over time to increase your profits. In my experience, it takes most real estate agents eighteen to twenty-four months to get to their target allocation percentages. Refer to the TAPs table below.

TABLE 29: TAPS REVIEW						
et Commission come Range	$0 – $250K	$250K – $500K	$500K – $1M	$1M – $5M	$5M – $10M	$10M – $50M
et Commission come	100%	100%	100%	100%	100%	100%
ofit	5%	10%	15%	20%	18%	17%
wner Pay	50%	35%	20%	10%	7%	3%
x	15%	15%	15%	15%	15%	15%
siness xpenses	30%	40%	50%	55%	60%	65%

If your net commission income is $800,000, you as the business owner would receive total owner pay of $160,000, or 20% of net commission income; profit would be $120,000, or 15%; tax would be $120,000, or 15%; and business expenses should be below $400,000, or 50%. Keep in mind, 20% owner pay is your after-tax pay. This is the amount of money deposited into your personal bank account.

Work the system long enough to achieve your target profitability. You were in business for a long time before you started Profit First for Real Estate Agents. You have some ingrained money habits that you'll need to replace. Focus on one improvement at a time. If you make too many changes at once, you may set yourself up for failure. Consistent focus on one thing at a time will win over any attempt to be a profit superhero making fifteen changes all at once.

Here are the general time frames you can take to build out your Profit First Rollout Plan:

- Four quarters
- Six quarters
- Eight quarters
- Twelve quarters

To determine the time frame you should choose, you will need to calculate your business expenses TAPs Gap. The business expenses TAPs Gap equals Target Business Expenses Percentage minus Current Business Expenses Percentage.

Look at your business expenses CAP. Now look at the TAP for business expenses in your net commission income range. Subtract your business expenses CAP from your business expenses TAP. This is your business expenses TAP Gap.

Here is an example of what that calculation looks like. Say you've completed your Instant Assessment with a net commission income range of $100,000 and are spending your money as follows:

Profit is $0 = 0%
Owner Pay is $30,000 = 30%
Tax is $10,000 = 10%
Business Expenses is $70,000 = 70%

The business expenses TAP for net commission income of $100,000 is 30%. Your business expenses CAP is 70%.

The business expenses TAP Gap is 70% − 30% = 40%.

Calculate how much you need to reduce your business expenses CAP each quarter, with each time frame. Divide your business expenses TAP Gap by the number of quarters you have in your Rollout Plan.

Four-Quarter Rollout Plan: 40% ÷ 4 quarters = 10% business expenses reduction for each quarter

Six-Quarter Rollout Plan: 40% ÷ 6 quarters = 6.7% business expenses reduction for each quarter

Eight-Quarter Rollout Plan: 40% ÷ 8 quarters = 5% business expenses reduction for each quarter

Twelve-Quarter Rollout Plan: 40% ÷ 12 quarters = 3% business expenses reduction for each quarter

If your business expenses TAP Gap is greater than 36%, choose a twelve-quarter Profit First Rollout Plan.

If your business expenses TAP Gap is greater than 20%, choose an eight-quarter Profit First Rollout Plan.

If your business expenses TAP Gap is from 10% to 20%, choose a six-quarter Profit First Rollout Plan.

If your business expenses TAP Gap is less than 10%, choose a four-quarter Profit First Rollout Plan.

The biggest thing to remember when you choose a Profit First Rollout Plan is to choose a plan you will sustain. You don't need to achieve profit superstardom overnight. It took some time to get where you are now. It will take some time to get your new profit results. It's easy to be overly optimistic about what we can accomplish in the short-term. You are implementing a new profitability system in your business. It will not be a perfect rollout. You will hit some roadblocks and obstacles along the way. Give yourself enough time and grace to be successful with your Profit First Rollout Plan.

Printed in the USA
CPSIA information can be obtained
at www.ICGtesting.com
LVHW090909240923
759168LV00007B/266